Beat
Binge
Drinking

A Smart Drinking Guide for Teens, College Students
and Young Adults Who Choose to Drink

Donna J. Cornett, M.A

People Friendly Books

Beat Binge Drinking

A Smart Drinking Guide for Teens, College Students
and Young Adults Who Choose to Drink

People Friendly Books

For information address:

People Friendly Books
P.O. Box 5441
Santa Rosa, CA 95402 USA
www.drinklinkmoderation.com

ISBN: 978-0-9763720-6-6

Library of Congress Control Number: 2010912597

Printed in the United States of America. 2010

To my baby sister, Dale, who died of alcoholism.
It didn't have to be that way.

Contents

Introduction

Did you know the earlier you start drinking, the more likely you'll become an alcoholic? That if you binge drink when you're young, you're also more likely to become an alcoholic? That most people establish lifelong patterns of alcohol use or abuse when they're young and young adults who drink heavily have more trouble adjusting to adulthood and to life in general? And that young drinkers have never had access to an alcohol harm reduction program teaching them safe drinking habits and attitudes, so they can avoid problem drinking?

Beat Binge Drinking is the first and only comprehensive alcohol abuse prevention program designed specifically for young adults - empowering them with moderate drinking tips and guidelines to reduce alcohol consumption and prevent problem drinking. It's a revolutionary breakthrough for drinkers and alcohol abuse treatment because it fills two huge voids - for the first time, it offers young people who choose to drink an attractive moderate drinking alternative and it also encourages them to proactively manage their alcohol use - instead of leaving it to chance or relying on parents, schools, laws or the community to do the job.

I've seen the effects of early binge drinking first hand. Since 1985, I've counseled thousands of problem drinkers - many started drinking and developed bad drinking habits at a very young age.

Some drinkers outgrew their bad habits, but most of the drinkers I talked to continued to go down hill and suffered the health, psychological, social, work, financial or legal consequences caused by alcohol abuse. That sparked my interest in underage and young adult drinking. I thought, instead of leaving drinking to a youngster's imagination, we should offer young people who were going to experiment with alcohol a realistic, moderate drinking program - teaching them what sensible drinking is and how to manage booze so it wouldn't ruin their lives. Then young adults wouldn't develop or be stuck with destructive problem drinking patterns for the rest of their lives, we could prevent alcohol abuse and we could reduce the alcoholism rate in this country and worldwide.

The more I looked into underage and young adult drinking, the more I became convinced there was a real need for such a program. For starters, young adult drinking is a leading public health and economic problem in the United States. In 2007 alone, young drinkers cost this country $68 billion in alcohol abuse treatment, medical care, work loss and pain and suffering. And every year, approximately 3.3 million young people between the ages of twelve and seventeen start drinking and join the ranks.

About 4,000 people in the United States die from alcohol poisoning every year and many of them are young people. Thousands of young drinkers are killed or injured in auto accidents, falls, fires, drownings, suicides and homicides because of alcohol abuse. And thousands ruin their lives and their futures because of it - never graduating from high school or college, getting into trouble with the law, racking up an arrest record, unable to hold down a job, having unplanned sex and children, having difficult relationships with family and friends and going into debt to pay off court fines, lawyer's fees and lawsuits. All because of binge or problem drinking.

Youngsters and young adults drink heavily and drink often. More than five million high school students - thirty-one percent of all high school students - say they binge at least once a month. Over half of these binge drinkers - one in four students - are frequent binge drinkers. They binge three or more times in a two week period.

Young people are starting to drink earlier too. In 1965, the average age a teen started drinking was seventeen and a half years, compared to age fourteen in 2003. The 2005 Monitoring the Future Study, an annual survey of U.S. youth, found three-fourths of 12th graders, more than two-thirds of 10th graders and about two in every five 8th graders have tried alcohol. Research also shows that kids who start drinking before the age of fifteen are five times more likely to become alcoholics at some time in their lives.

College presidents say binge drinking is the most serious problem they face on campus. Forty-three percent or two in five college students are binge drinkers consuming five or more drinks at a time. And over half of the college students who drink, say they drink to get drunk.

If you're a college binge drinker, you're more likely to miss class, fall behind in school, damage property, get hurt in alcohol-related accidents, engage in unplanned, unprotected sexual activity and get in trouble with campus police. You're also more likely to argue with friends and get behind the wheel when you've been drinking.

Every year almost 500,000 college students suffer from alcohol-related injuries and 1400 die from them. About 400,000 students have unprotected sex and more than 100,000 say they've been too drunk to know if they consented to having sex. Almost 100,000 are victims of alcohol-related sexual assault or date rape. And close to 150,000 have alcohol-related health problems. Twenty-five percent have academic problems because of drinking, eleven percent say they have damaged property when under the influence, five percent have had run-ins with police and the law because of booze and approximately four million college students drive drunk every year.

Non-drinking students, as well as the surrounding community, also suffer the consequences of alcohol abuse among young people - increased crime, traffic accidents, rapes, property damage and assaults.

Alcohol is clearly the drug of choice for teenagers and college students. It's legal, cheap, socially acceptable, easy to get and the effects are immediate. A 2002 report by Columbia University's National Center on Addiction and Substance Abuse (CASA) shows eighty-one percent of high school students have tried alcohol, compared to seventy percent who have tried tobacco and forty-seven percent who have tried marijuana. And kids who experiment with alcohol tend to keep using it. Girls are now drinking almost as much as boys. And beer is the drink of choice for binge drinkers - accounting for more than eighty percent of excessive alcohol consumption in the United States. Sixty-three percent of beer drinkers under the age of twenty-four report binge drinking.

Even though liquor is a fact of life and we live in an alcohol-saturated culture, until now, teaching kids how to handle it has been off limits. To many people, just acknowledging that young people drink implies you condone or promote it. In fact, most parents, teachers and psychologists are afraid of the subject and think if they bring it up they'll be encouraging drinking. The truth is most teens and young adults will experiment with booze sooner or later whether we like it or not - just like they experiment with sex and driving. So it's time to stop ignoring or avoiding the problem and start teaching young people moderate drinking habits and attitudes early on, just like we teach them about safe sex and how to drive a car.

Why is it so important to offer a moderate drinking program specifically for young adults? Because young people drink for different reasons than mature adults. They're making the difficult transition from adolescence to adulthood - physiologically and psychologically - and assuming many more new responsibilities. Competition is fierce and many adolescents strive to be perfect - look great, get good grades, be athletic and the most popular person in school. They also face intense peer pressure, self-esteem problems, they worry about their future, they're stressed about going to college or getting a job and they may also have family or financial problems. Most adults, on the other hand, drink and binge for different reasons. Another fact to support an alcohol abuse prevention program designed just for young people.

And even though there's no question the younger you start drinking and the more you drink when you're young, the more trouble you'll have with alcohol when you're an adult, drinking prevention programs for kids in this country have been limited to environmental and individual-focused approaches. Environmental interventions include increasing the price or taxes on alcohol, increasing the minimum drinking age and enforcing it, instituting policies and training servers of alcoholic beverages to prevent sales to underage or intoxicated patrons, enacting zero tolerance laws that make it illegal for people under twenty-one to drive after any drinking and increasing law enforcement of alcohol sellers and buyers. And individual-focused interventions include family-based, school-based and community-based prevention programs which provide information about the dangers of alcohol, address peer pressure to drink and how to handle it, set rules against drinking, enforce non-drinking rules and monitor an adolescent's behavior to avoid alcohol use. Many of these approaches tell youngsters to "just say no" to alcohol which doesn't work. In fact, it might make kids even more curious and more likely to abuse alcohol. And none of these approaches teach what moderate drinking is or encourage the young drinker to assume responsibility and take charge of their alcohol use.

Obviously, current approaches aren't effective because binge and problem drinking among young people are on the rise. Even the National Institute on Alcohol Abuse and Alcoholism recognizes there's a major unmet need that exists in alcohol abuse treatment for teens, college students and young adults.

Beat Binge Drinking fills that need by offering young people who choose to drink a smart, realistic guide to alcohol use - teaching them what moderate drinking is and encouraging them to proactively manage their drinking. It's an attractive harm reduction program designed to prevent problem drinking and alcoholism that respects the young drinker's intelligence and individuality and makes them responsible for their drinking behavior.

Personally and professionally, I think young people should avoid drinking alcohol for as long as they can. If you don't drink, great! But if you do drink, arm yourself with Beat Binge Drinking and drink wisely.

Take Care,

Donna Cornett
Founder and Director
Drink/Link Moderate Drinking Programs and Products

Disclaimer

The guidelines, tips and exercises in this book are not recommended for the alcoholic, anyone who has a serious drinking problem, anyone who has a physical or psychological condition caused or aggravated by alcohol use, anyone who suffers from serious health, psychological, social, legal, financial or job-related problems as a result of alcohol use, any woman who is pregnant or thinking of becoming pregnant or anyone who has successfully abstained. This book does not advocate or encourage anyone who is under the legal drinking age of twenty-one to drink alcohol. Results vary according to the individual.

Part I:
Get Ready, Get Set, Get Smart!

Chapter One:
What's the Beat Binge
Drinking Program All About?

You're Special!

You're special whether you know it or not. The Beat Binge Drinking Program was designed just for you - teens, college students and young adults.

If you're reading this book and working the program because you want to, congratulations! You're smart enough to know it's time to do something about your drinking. You care about yourself and where you're headed in life and you're ready to replace problem drinking with smart drinking. You're probably a highly intelligent, independent-minded individual who likes taking charge, instead of sitting around and waiting for things to happen. You're special and you've got the drive to make smart drinking happen.

But if you're reading this book and working the program because someone else wants you to - a good friend, parent, relative, teacher, doctor, counselor, psychologist or clergyman - you're also special! The person who referred you to this program recognizes how great you are and they care about you so much they want you to clean up your act. Lucky you! You've got a guardian angel looking over you with your best interests at heart - trying to help you avoid the pitfalls in life. What more could you ask for?

BTW, you don't have to be a binge drinker to benefit from the Beat Binge Drinking Program. Maybe you can't decide if alcohol is for you and the information in this book will help you make up your mind. Maybe you're new to the drinking scene; you don't want to leave your drinking to chance and want to feel confident that if you do drink, you won't harm yourself or others. Maybe a cool adult gave you this guide to educate you about liquor before you start drinking, so you don't abuse it. They want you to know what moderate drinking is and how to stick to drink limits before you even start. Or maybe your friends gave you this book because they've observed you drinking and they're worried about the toll booze is taking on you.

And even though this program was designed for young binge drinkers, you'll find many of the sensible drinking suggestions offered here useful for fixing other drinking problems too. Problem drinking comes in many different forms and binge drinking is just one of them. So if you don't consider yourself a binge drinker, but sometimes think you drink too much, too often, for the wrong reasons or you have other problems because of alcohol, you can still benefit from this program.

Regardless of how you got your hands on this book and whatever your motivation is for working the Beat Binge Drinking Program, the moderate drinking guidelines and tips you learn here should serve you well, not only when you're young, but for the rest of your life. Learn them, practice them and own them and you'll never worry about alcohol or drinking again.

What Can You Expect From This Program?

If you complete this program and continue to practice everything you learn, you can expect to learn smart drinking habits and attitudes, to reduce your alcohol consumption, to eliminate binge or problem drinking and to prevent alcoholism. Alcohol will become less important to you, you'll put it in perspective and you'll develop a healthier relationship with it. You'll drink moderately and appropriately and you won't rely on liquor for entertainment, social acceptance or to cope with feelings or moods.

Beat Binge Drinking is based on a harm reduction philosophy - if you choose to drink, the goal is to reduce your risk of alcohol abuse and all of the health, psychological, social, school, work, financial and legal problems associated with it. It's a realistic approach that recognizes you may experiment with alcohol, even though you may be underage and your parents and society don't approve of it. It doesn't underestimate you and trusts you'll make the right decisions about alcohol, once you're educated about it. It also believes you're capable of change - of uniearning binge or problem drinking habits and replacing them with smart, healthy ones. And you're totally responsible for your behavior, including your drinking behavior - nobody else is.

Beat Binge Drinking is a positive, intelligent guide to alcohol use designed just for you. It respects you, your intelligence and your individuality. It gives you the facts about alcohol use and abuse. And it teaches you how to drink smart - empowering you with sensible drinking skills and strategies so you don't harm yourself or others.

<u>What Can You Expect From the Beat Binge Drinking Program?</u>

- *You'll learn smart drinking habits and attitudes*
- *You'll reduce your alcohol consumption*
- *You'll eliminate binge or problem drinking*
- *You'll prevent alcoholism*

How Can You Get the Most Out of This Program?

There are three things you can do to get the most out of this program. The first thing is to get involved! Be proactive, question why you drink and ask yourself how you can handle people, places, feelings and circumstances without booze. Be proactive with the smart drinking guidelines and tips you'll learn too. Apply each one of them to your life and your drinking behavior. You'll find out if a smart drinking suggestion works for you - helps you to stay within your drink limit - if you practice it at least two times. If it does, keep it in your repertoire of moderate drinking skills. It will be at your command for the rest of your life. And remember - smart drinking concepts and techniques are just words on paper unless you put them to good use.

The second thing you can do to get the most out of this program is to take your time and concentrate on only one chapter a week. Every chapter is loaded with ideas and tips. If you read the whole book in one day, you'll be overwhelmed and won't know where to start. Stick to just one chapter a week, get into it, do what it says to do and you'll get the most out of the program.

The third thing you can do to get the most out of the program is to complete the teaser at the end of most chapters. A teaser is an exercise designed to help you gain insight into why, when, where and how you drink. And the more insight you have about your drinking, the less you'll engage in mindless, destructive drinking. The teasers will also help keep you on track, raise your drinking awareness and lower your alcohol consumption - naturally. Do them!

Get involved, stick to just one chapter a week and do the teaser at the end of most chapters and you'll make a change for the better.

How Can You Get the Most Out of the Beat Binge Drinking Program?

- *Get involved and be proactive*
- *Apply the moderate drinking strategies and skills you learn to your life and your drinking behavior*
- *Concentrate on only one chapter a week*
- *Complete the teaser each week*

Chapter Two:
What Is Binge Drinking?

Knowledge is power. Learn what binge drinking, alcohol abuse and alcoholism are, what happens to you when you're under the influence and how high you get with different doses of alcohol. The more knowledge you have about booze, the more power you'll have to control it.

Binge Drinking Is . . .

Binge drinking is a form of problem drinking that often leads to alcoholism. Loosely defined, binge drinking is drinking to get drunk. More precisely, the United States Department of Health and Human Service's National Institute on Alcohol Abuse and Alcoholism (NIAAA) defines binge drinking as a drinking pattern which raises your blood alcohol concentration (BAC) to .08 gram percent or above, which translates into five or more drinks for males over a two hour period and four or more drinks for females over a two hour period. Your BAC is the amount of alcohol in your bloodstream.

The Harvard University School of Public Health College Alcohol Study (CAS) goes a little further and considers men and women who drink in this manner once or twice within a two-week period to be occasional binge drinkers. And those who drink in this manner three or more times within a two-week period to be frequent binge drinkers.

Keep in mind, binge drinking is not "risky" drinking - which is getting pretty high and reaching a BAC of between .05 and .08. It's also not a "bender" - which is two or more days in a row of heavy drinking. And don't think you're out of the woods and you don't have a drinking problem if you have fewer than four or five drinks in a row. Just because you don't drink that much in one sitting doesn't necessarily mean you don't have a drinking problem. You can drink less and still get into trouble with alcohol.

FYI - one drink is considered twelve ounces of beer, five ounces of wine or one and a half ounces of hard liquor. Don't forget the legal age to drink alcohol is twenty-one and it's illegal to drink if you're under twenty-one. And if you're at risk for alcoholism, you increase that risk with any alcohol consumption.

<u>Binge Drinking Is . . .</u>

- *Men having five or more drinks in a row and reaching a .08 BAC or higher in two hours*
- *Women having four or more drinks in a row and reaching a .08 BAC or higher in two hours*

<u>One Drink Is . . .</u>

- *One twelve ounce beer*
- *One five ounce glass of wine*
- *One and a half ounces of hard liquor*

Alcohol Abuse Is . . .

Alcohol abuse is problem drinking and it comes in many different forms. It can be binge drinking, habitual drinking, stress-related drinking or emotional drinking that causes health, psychological, relationship, school, work, legal or financial problems for you.

If you suffer from hangovers, blackouts or alcohol-related health problems, you have relationship difficulties because of booze, you fail to fulfill major responsibilities at home, school or work because you'd rather drink, you expose yourself to dangerous situations when you're under the influence - like drinking and driving - you have legal problems because of alcohol - like getting arrested for drunk driving or public drunkenness - or you can't pay your bills because you spend your money on beer and you continue to drink in spite of these problems, you're an alcohol abuser or problem drinker.

Take note - you don't have to suffer from all of these symptoms to be a problem drinker. If you can identify with just one or two, you should consider yourself a problem drinker.

Symptoms of Alcohol Abuse or Problem Drinking

- *You suffer from hangovers, blackouts or alcohol-related health problems*
- *You have difficult relationships because of alcohol*
- *You're unable to fulfill major responsibilities because of alcohol*
- *You expose yourself to dangerous situations when drinking, like drinking and driving*
- *You have legal problems because of alcohol*
- *You have financial problems because of alcohol*
- *You continue to drink in spite of alcohol-related problems*

Alcoholism Is . . .

Alcoholism is alcohol addiction or dependence and it also takes many different forms. If you get drunk "just on the weekends", you can be an alcoholic. If you "just drink beer", you can be an alcoholic. If you drink secretly, you can be an alcoholic. You don't have to be in the gutter to be an alcoholic.

You may suffer from many of the same symptoms associated with alcohol abuse - you have hangovers, blackouts or alcohol-related health problems, relationship problems, you don't fulfill important home, work or school obligations, you do dangerous things when you drink, you break the law when you're under the influence or you don't pay your bills - and you continue to drink in spite of these problems. But you're an alcoholic if you have strong cravings for alcohol, you can't control your drinking and you're unable to stop once you've started, you have a very high tolerance to alcohol - you need a lot to get high - and you suffer from withdrawal symptoms, like headaches, restlessness and irritability, if you don't drink.

You don't have to suffer from all of these symptoms to be an alcoholic. If you suffer from just three, you are an alcoholic.

Symptoms of Alcoholism

- *You suffer from hangovers, blackouts or alcohol-related health problems*
- *You have difficult relationships because of alcohol*
- *You're unable to fulfill major responsibilities because of alcohol*
- *You expose yourself to dangerous situations when drinking, like drinking and driving*
- *You have legal problems because of alcohol*
- *You have financial problems because of alcohol*
- *You have a strong craving for alcohol*
- *You can't stop drinking once you start*
- *You have a very high tolerance to alcohol*
- *You suffer from withdrawal symptoms if you don't drink*
- *You continue to drink in spite of alcohol-related problems*

What Happens When You Get High?

Here's a blow-by-blow description of how you think and feel at different blood alcohol concentration (BAC) levels in your body over a one hour period.

Between .02 and .05 BAC - one or two drinks for a 160-pound man or one drink for a 120-pound woman over one hour - you feel relaxed and happy. You may also become more talkative and feel less inhibited - into communicating your feelings and thoughts. Your reaction time, decision making and judgment skills can all become impaired at a mere .04 BAC!

Between .05 and .06 BAC - two drinks for a 160-pound man or a little more than one drink for a 120-pound woman over one hour - and your emotions and behavior start to become exaggerated. You feel even better - warmer, mildly sedated and your vision and hearing also become impaired. Loss of motor coordination begins at around .05 BAC and your memory becomes mildly impaired.

Between .07 and .09 BAC - three drinks for a 160-pound man or less than two drinks for a 120-pound woman over one hour - and your speech, balance, coordination and reflexes are all impaired. You feel light-headed, giddy and even less inhibited. Your judgment, reasoning, memory and reaction time are all affected, but you may not be aware of it. A .08 BAC is considered binge drinking and legally drunk in most states.

Between .10 and .13 BAC - more than four drinks for a 160-pound man and less than three drinks for a 120-pound woman over one hour - and your balance, coordination, reaction time, judgment and memory become even more impaired. You become more susceptible to mood swings and may feel very happy, very sad or very angry. You slur your words and stagger.

Between .14 and .17 BAC - about six to seven drinks for a 160-pound man and less than four drinks for a 120-pound woman over one hour - and you experience major physical and mental problems. Talking and standing become difficult. Perception and judgment are distorted and you don't comprehend how out of it you are. Blackouts can occur.

Between .20 and .25 BAC - less than nine drinks for a 160-pound man and a little more than five drinks for a 120-pound woman over one hour - and you become dazed and confused. You're in a stupor and cannot function without assistance.

Between .30 and .35 BAC - more than ten drinks for a 160-pound man and eight drinks for a 120-pound woman over one hour - and your perception, cognition and comprehension are almost non-existent. You pass out, become unconscious and vital reflexes, like breathing and gagging, become suppressed. You can choke to death on your own vomit, spontaneously stop breathing or die from alcohol poisoning at this point.

At .40 BAC you become unconscious and death is imminent.

Alcohol is a powerful drug. Respect it if you use it. Tune into the physiological and psychological changes going on in your body and brain the next time you tip your glass. You might drink less.

Blood Alcohol Concentration Charts

Here are two Blood Alcohol Concentration (BAC) charts to help you calculate how high you get when you drink. The text BAC chart is courtesy of the California Driver Handbook and the numeric BAL (Blood Alcohol Level) chart is compliments of Colorado State University.

If you weigh between 90 and 109 pounds:

- And it has been 1 hour or less since your first drink and you consume 1 drink, your BAC is probably between .05% and .07%.
- And it has been 1 hour or less since your first drink and you consume 2 or more drinks, your BAC is probably .08% or higher.

- And it has been 2 hours or less since your first drink and you consume 1 drink, your BAC is probably between .01% and .04%.
- And it has been 2 hours or less since your first drink and you consume 2 drinks, your BAC is probably between .05% and .07%.
- And it has been 2 hours or less since your first drink and you consume 3 or more drinks, your BAC is probably .08% or higher.
- And it has been 3 hours or less since your first drink and you consume 1 drink, your BAC is probably between .01% and .04%.
- And it has been 3 hours or less since your first drink and you consume 2 drinks, your BAC is probably between .05% and .07%.
- And it has been 3 hours or less since your first drink and you consume 3 or more drinks, your BAC is probably .08% or higher.
- And it has been 4 hours or less since your first drink and you consume 1 drink, your BAC is probably between .01% and .04%.
- And it has been 4 hours or less since your first drink and you consume 2 drinks, your BAC is probably between .05% and .07%.
- And it has been 4 hours or less since your first drink and you consume 3 or more drinks, your BAC is probably .08% or higher.

If you weigh between 110 and 129 pounds:

- And it has been 1 hour or less since your first drink and you consume 1 drink, your BAC is probably between .05% and .07%.

- And it has been 1 hour or less since your first drink and you consume 2 or more drinks, your BAC is probably .08% or higher.
- And it has been 2 hours or less since your first drink and you consume 1 drink, your BAC is probably between .01% and .04%.
- And it has been 2 hours or less since your first drink and you consume 2 drinks, your BAC is probably between .05% and .07%.
- And it has been 2 hours or less since your first drink and you consume 3 or more drinks, your BAC is probably .08% or higher.
- And it has been 3 hours or less since your first drink and you consume 1 drink, your BAC is probably between .01% and .04%.
- And it has been 3 hours or less since your first drink and you consume 2 drinks, your BAC is probably between .05% and .07%.
- And it has been 3 hours or less since your first drink and you consume 3 or more drinks, your BAC is probably .08% or higher.
- And it has been 4 hours or less since your first drink and you consume 2 drinks, your BAC is probably between .01% and .04%.
- And it has been 4 hours or less since your first drink and you consume 3 drinks, your BAC is probably between .05% and .07%.
- And it has been 4 hours or less since your first drink and you consume 4 or more drinks, your BAC is probably .08% or higher.

If you weigh between 130 and 149 pounds:

- And it has been 1 hour or less since your first drink and you consume 1 drink, your BAC is probably between .01% and .04%.
- And it has been 1 hour or less since your first drink and you consume 2 drinks, your BAC is probably between .05% and .07%
- And it has been 1 hour or less since your first drink and you consume 3 or more drinks, your BAC is probably .08% or higher.
- And it has been 2 hours or less since your first drink and you consume 1 or more drink, your BAC is probably between .01% and .04%.
- And it has been 2 hours or less since your first drink and you consume 2 drinks, your BAC is probably between .05% and .07%.
- And it has been 2 hours or less since your first drink and you consume 3 or more drinks, your BAC is probably .08% or higher.
- And it has been 3 hours or less since your first drink and you consume 2 drinks, your BAC is probably between .01% and .04%.
- And it has been 3 hours or less since your first drink and you consume 3 drinks, your BAC is probably between .05% and .07%.
- And it has been 3 hours or less since your first drink and you consume 4 or more drinks, your BAC is probably .08% or higher.
- And it has been 4 hours or less since your first drink and you consume 2 drinks, your BAC is probably between .01% and .04%.

- And it has been 4 hours or less since your first drink and you consume 3 drinks, your BAC is probably between .05% and .07%.
- And it has been 4 hours or less since your first drink and you consume 4 or more drinks, your BAC is probably .08% or higher.

If you weigh between 150 and 169 pounds:

- And it has been 1 hour or less since your first drink and you consume 1 drink, your BAC is probably between .01% and .04%.
- And it has been 1 hour or less since your first drink and you consume 2 drinks, your BAC is probably between .05% and .07%
- And it has been 1 hour or less since your first drink and you consume 3 or more drinks, your BAC is probably .08% or higher.
- And it has been 2 hours or less since your first drink and you consume 1 drink, your BAC is probably between .01% and .04%.
- And it has been 2 hours or less since your first drink and you consume 3 drinks, your BAC is probably between .05% and .07%.
- And it has been 2 hours or less since your first drink and you consume 4 or more drinks, your BAC is probably .08% or higher.
- And it has been 3 hours or less since your first drink and you consume 2 drinks, your BAC is probably between .01% and .04%.
- And it has been 3 hours or less since your first drink and you consume 3 drinks, your BAC is probably between .05% and .07%.

- And it has been 3 hours or less since your first drink and you consume 4 or more drinks, your BAC is probably .08% or higher.
- And it has been 4 hours or less since your first drink and you consume 3 drinks, your BAC is probably between .01% and .04%.
- And it has been 4 hours or less since your first drink and you consume 4 drinks, your BAC is probably between .05% and .07%.
- And it has been 4 hours or less since your first drink and you consume 5 or more drinks, your BAC is probably .08% or higher

If you weigh between 170 and 189 pounds:

- And it has been 1 hour or less since your first drink and you consume 1 drink, your BAC is probably between .01% and .04%.
- And it has been 1 hour or less since your first drink and you consume 2 drinks, your BAC is probably between .05% and .07%
- And it has been 1 hour or less since your first drink and you consume 3 or more drinks, your BAC is probably .08% or higher.
- And it has been 2 hours or less since your first drink and you consume 2 drinks, your BAC is probably between .01% and .04%.
- And it has been 2 hours or less since your first drink and you consume 3 drinks, your BAC is probably between .05% and .07%.
- And it has been 2 hours or less since your first drink and you consume 4 or more drinks, your BAC is probably .08% or higher.

- And it has been 3 hours or less since your first drink and you consume 2 drinks, your BAC is probably between .01% and .04%.
- And it has been 3 hours or less since your first drink and you consume 4 drinks, your BAC is probably between .05% and .07%.
- And it has been 3 hours or less since your first drink and you consume 5 or more drinks, your BAC is probably .08% or higher.
- And it has been 4 hours or less since your first drink and you consume 3 drinks, your BAC is probably between .01% and .04%.
- And it has been 4 hours or less since your first drink and you consume 4 drinks, your BAC is probably between .05% and .07%.
- And it has been 4 hours or less since your first drink and you consume 6 or more drinks, your BAC is probably .08% or higher

If you weigh between 190 and 209 pounds:

- And it has been 1 hour or less since your first drink and you consume 1 drink, your BAC is probably between .01% and .04%.
- And it has been 1 hour or less since your first drink and you consume 3 drinks, your BAC is probably between .05% and .07%
- And it has been 1 hour or less since your first drink and you consume 4 or more drinks, your BAC is probably .08% or higher.
- And it has been 2 hours or less since your first drink and you consume 2 drinks, your BAC is probably between .01% and .04%.

- And it has been 2 hours or less since your first drink and you consume 4 drinks, your BAC is probably between .05% and .07%.
- And it has been 2 hours or less since your first drink and you consume 5 or more drinks, your BAC is probably .08% or higher.
- And it has been 3 hours or less since your first drink and you consume 3 drinks, your BAC is probably between .01% and .04%.
- And it has been 3 hours or less since your first drink and you consume 4 drinks, your BAC is probably between .05% and .07%.
- And it has been 3 hours or less since your first drink and you consume 5 or more drinks, your BAC is probably .08% or higher.
- And it has been 4 hours or less since your first drink and you consume 4 drinks, your BAC is probably between .01% and .04%.
- And it has been 4 hours or less since your first drink and you consume 5 drinks, your BAC is probably between .05% and .07%.
- And it has been 4 hours or less since your first drink and you consume 6 or more drinks, your BAC is probably .08% or higher

If you weigh 210 or more pounds:

- And it has been 1 hour or less since your first drink and you consume 1 drink, your BAC is probably between .01% and .04%.
- And it has been 1 hour or less since your first drink and you consume 3 drinks, your BAC is probably between .05% and .07%

- And it has been 1 hour or less since your first drink and you consume 4 or more drinks, your BAC is probably .08% or higher.
- And it has been 2 hours or less since your first drink and you consume 2 drinks, your BAC is probably between .01% and .04%.
- And it has been 2 hours or less since your first drink and you consume 4 drinks, your BAC is probably between .05% and .07%.
- And it has been 2 hours or less since your first drink and you consume 5 or more drinks, your BAC is probably .08% or higher.
- And it has been 3 hours or less since your first drink and you consume 3 drinks, your BAC is probably between .01% and .04%.
- And it has been 3 hours or less since your first drink and you consume 5 drinks, your BAC is probably between .05% and .07%.
- And it has been 3 hours or less since your first drink and you consume 6 or more drinks, your BAC is probably .08% or higher.
- And it has been 4 hours or less since your first drink and you consume 4 drinks, your BAC is probably between .01% and .04%.
- And it has been 4 hours or less since your first drink and you consume 6 drinks, your BAC is probably between .05% and .07%.
- And it has been 4 hours or less since your first drink and you consume 7 or more drinks, your BAC is probably .08% or higher.

Men's B.A.L. Estimation Chart

Drinks	100	120	140	160	180	200	220	240	
0	.00	.00	.00	.00	.00	.00	.00	.00	Only Safe Driving Limit
1	.04	.03	.03	.02	.02	.02	.02	.02	
2	.08	.06	.05	.05	.04	.04	.03	.03	Driving Skills Impaired
3	.11	.09	.08	.07	.06	.06	.05	.05	
4	.15	.12	.11	.09	.08	.08	.07	.06	
5	.19	.16	.13	.12	.11	.09	.09	.08	
6	.23	.19	.16	.14	.13	.11	.10	.09	
7	.26	.22	.19	.16	.15	.13	.12	.11	Legally Intoxicated
8	.30	.25	.21	.19	.17	.15	.14	.13	
9	.34	.28	.24	.21	.19	.17	.15	.14	
10	.38	.31	.27	.23	.21	.19	.17	.16	Possible Death

1 drink equals roughly 1.5 ounces of 80 proof hard alcohol or 1 ounce of 100 proof hard alcohol, 1 12oz. beer, or 1 5oz. glass of wine.

Women's B.A.L. Estimation Chart

Drinks	100	120	140	160	180	200	220	240	
0	.00	.00	.00	.00	.00	.00	.00	.00	Only Safe Driving Limit
1	.05	.04	.03	.03	.03	.02	.02	.02	
2	.09	.08	.07	.06	.05	.05	.04	.04	Driving Skills Impaired
3	.14	.11	.10	.09	.08	.07	.06	.06	
4	.18	.15	.13	.11	.10	.09	.08	.08	
5	.23	.19	.16	.14	.13	.11	.10	.09	
6	.27	.23	.19	.17	.15	.14	.12	.11	
7	.32	.27	.23	.20	.18	.16	.14	.13	Legally Intoxicated
8	.36	.30	.26	.23	.20	.18	.17	.15	
9	.41	.34	.29	.26	.23	.20	.19	.17	
10	.45	.38	.32	.28	.25	.23	.21	.19	Possible Death

1 drink equals roughly 1.5 ounces of 80 proof hard alcohol or 1 ounce of 100 proof hard alcohol, 1 12oz. beer, or 1 5oz. glass of wine.

Teaser

How high do you get when you have one drink in one hour, two drinks in one hour, three drinks in one hour, four drinks in one hour, five drinks in one hour? Record all of these BAC's. How many drinks put you at .08 BAC in one hour? Record that number.

How high do you get when you have one drink in two hours, two drinks in two hours, three drinks in two hours, four drinks in two hours, five drinks in two hours? Record all of these BAC's. How many drinks put you at .08 BAC in two hours? Record that number.

How high do you get when you have one drink in three hours, two drinks in three hours, three drinks in three hours, four drinks in three hours, five drinks in three hours? Record all of these BAC's. How many drinks put you at .08 BAC in three hours? Record that number.

How high do you get when you have one drink in four hours, two drinks in four hours, three drinks in four hours, four drinks in four hours, five drinks in four hours? Record all of these BAC's. How many drinks put you at .08 BAC in four hours? Record that number.

Know your limits!

Chapter Three:
How Does Binge Drinking
Affect You Physically?

Here's more info on how alcohol and binge drinking affect your body and brain. Just the facts so you can make informed decisions about drinking.

Short-Term Physical Effects of Binge Drinking

Alcohol is a central nervous system depressant you absorb into your bloodstream through your stomach and small intestine. It is metabolized or broken down in your liver, but your liver can only metabolize a small amount of alcohol at a time, so the rest of it circulates throughout your body making you high.

Gender, age, race, health, ethnicity, food, how fast you drink, if you take other drugs or medications and family influences can all factor in to how you metabolize liquor. Most people break down about one ounce of alcohol - the amount of alcohol in one drink - in one hour. So if you have more than one drink per hour, the booze accumulates in your body and you can become intoxicated.

If you binge and quickly gulp one drink after another, you get high fast. You feel relaxed and euphoric within minutes and you want to maintain this high, so you keep on guzzling. Soon you hit or exceed .08 BAC and you're wasted.

Getting drunk is the most obvious short-term effect of bingeing. You lose control of your body and have difficulty walking and talking. You lose control of your brain too. You're unable to reason or exercise good judgment. And you can't make sound decisions about anything, including drinking.

The next most obvious short-term symptom of bingeing is the blackout - you appear to be conscious while you're drinking, but you have no memory the next day of events that took place when you were under the influence. You forgot what you said and did when you were drunk and when people refresh your memory about your behavior the night before, you're often ashamed and embarrassed.

Bingeing actually erases your memory for periods of time. A blackout is really alcohol-induced brain damage and it occurs when you drink a lot of liquor over a short period of time. Electrical shocks and concussions can also cause blackouts. However, when you have an alcohol-induced blackout, you're more likely to engage in risky behavior. Research shows students experiencing blackouts get involved in a wide range of dangerous activities - from drunk driving, to getting into fights, to having unplanned, unprotected sex, to vandalizing property, to spending lots of money - and they have no recollection of what they did the next day.

Even if you don't have a total memory loss, as you would with a blackout, bingeing can cause other memory problems. Minor events or large periods of time may be completely erased from your memory when you binge. These events were never really recorded in your brain in the first place because alcohol and acetaldehyde, a chemical which is produced when alcohol is metabolized in your liver, destroy the cells in your brain associated with long-term memory. Since your brain never recorded these memories, you'll never recover them.

The third most obvious symptom of bingeing is the hangover. The pounding headache, upset stomach, vomiting, diarrhea, irritability and fatigue. You feel like you have the flu, but booze, not a virus, is to blame. You're physically and mentally "off" - the lining of your digestive system, your organs and your brain have all been affected by alcohol and you feel like you've been hit by a truck.

A hangover is actually a sign of alcohol withdrawal and it happens after heavy or prolonged drinking. Your body adjusted to the presence of booze when you were drinking and now it's trying to adjust to the absence of it - and you're paying the price. A bad hangover can keep you in bed for days. And a mild one makes you tired - you drag yourself through the day. No wonder you feel like skipping class or calling in sick to work when you're hung over.

Too much sauce can also cause sleeping problems. Alcohol reduces the important REM phase of sleep and the less REM sleep you get, the less likely you'll fall into a deep sleep. So, in addition to being hung over, you're also sleep deprived. A miserable combination.

Last but not least, alcohol poisoning and death can result from binge drinking. Even though liquor is legal, cheap, convenient and socially acceptable, in large quantities it's lethal. Too much and your reflexes and vital functions don't work and your body shuts down. Approximately 4,000 Americans die from alcohol poisoning every year and many of them are young people.

Keep in mind these are just the short-term physiological problems associated with binge or problem drinking. They don't include the health, psychological, relationship, social, school, work, legal or financial problems caused by it.

<u>Short-Term Physical Effects of Binge Drinking</u>

- *You get high*
- *You become impaired physically and mentally*
- *You get drunk*
- *You blackout*
- *Memories are erased or not formed*
- *You have a hangover*
- *You have problems sleeping*
- *You suffer or die from alcohol poisoning*

Long-Term Physical Effects of Binge Drinking

Alcohol affects your entire body. It's like poison and it damages your cells, tissues and organs. Your body tries hard to eliminate it. About five percent of the booze in your bloodstream is excreted through your lungs, sweat, saliva and urine and the rest is removed by your liver.

Your liver does the heavy lifting so it's no wonder it's one the first organs to go if you drink too much. Alcohol abuse causes fat to build up in your liver and this fat accumulates, crowds out and eventually kills other healthy liver cells. The organ becomes tender, swollen and inflamed - a condition known as alcoholic hepatitis. If you stop or cut down on your drinking and eat well, this condition is reversible. But if you continue to binge, scar tissue forms in the organ which leads to irreversible cirrhosis of the liver which can be deadly.

Your pancreas is another casualty of alcohol abuse. Binge or problem drinking can lead to pancreatitis, a dangerous condition where the pancreas becomes inflamed. It causes severe pain in the upper abdomen, lower chest and back along with nausea, vomiting and constipation. It can also be life-threatening.

The rest of your digestive system is also on the hit list. Liquor can weaken and inflame the lining of your stomach, a condition known as gastritis, which causes nausea, indigestion, vomiting, bloating, diarrhea, headache and internal bleeding. Stomach and intestinal ulcers can also develop in heavy drinkers. Plus, you can become susceptible to alcoholic muscle damage which destroys your body's ability to absorb and metabolize nutrients essential for good health. And if you can't get the nutrients you need to live, you waste away and starve to death.

Your heart can also be a binge drinking casualty. Alcohol and acetaldehyde, a chemical your body produces when you metabolize alcohol, can damage your heart and lead to alcoholic cardiomyopathy, which causes palpitations and difficulty breathing. An abnormal heartbeat and high blood pressure are also symptoms of heavy drinking and can lead to heart failure. More deadly conditions caused by alcohol abuse.

Booze can actually shrink your brain and brain activity slows in people who drink too much. Alcohol-induced brain damage occurs in the prefrontal cortex of the brain, the part of your brain that helps you make plans, make decisions, control impulses and stay focused. If you suffer from brain damage in this area of your brain, you probably have a short attention span and you're unable to concentrate, get organized, make decisions, control impulses or complete tasks. You lack self-discipline and your memory and ability to learn are impaired. Too much alcohol can also increase your risk of developing dementia later in life.

Research shows your brain continues to develop throughout adolescence and into young adulthood and many scientists are concerned that drinking during this critical developmental period may lead to lifelong impairments in brain functions, especially memory, motor skills and coordination. Adolescent bingeing can affect your brain function for the rest of your life.

You increase your risk of getting cancer when you drink too. Head, neck, liver, lung, mouth, throat, larynx, esophagus, colon, bladder and esophageal cancers have all been linked to heavy drinking.

Malnutrition also develops in problem drinkers and alcoholics because liquor hinders digestion and your body's ability to make important nutrients necessary for cells and vital organs. Malnutrition can cause mental confusion, emotional instability, fatigue, memory loss, irritability, nerve damage, hallucinations, vision problems and brain hemorrhaging.

Alcohol is toxic to bone marrow that makes red blood cells. And when your body produces fewer red blood cells, you become anemic and feel weak and tired. Anemia also weakens your immune system and makes you more susceptible to other health problems.

Bleeding becomes a concern if you drink too much. Chronic, heavy alcohol use can cause ulcers in your stomach and small intestine and when they become irritated by alcohol, they bleed. Sometimes medication can control the bleeding. Sometimes internal bleeding requires surgery. Sometimes drinkers die from internal bleeding doctors can't stop.

And drinking when you're young can actually stunt your growth. Alcohol prevents calcium absorption in your body to build healthy bones. It also weakens muscle fiber and reduces the production of proteins which prevent normal cell growth - ultimately leading to muscle damage. So much for strong bones and muscles if you binge.

You can develop a high tolerance to alcohol when you overdo it on a regular basis too. The more you drink, the longer you drink, the higher your tolerance is to alcohol. If you develop a high tolerance for liquor, your body and brain have become accustomed to it so you need more and more to get high - a bad sign of physical addiction to booze.

Withdrawal symptoms are more serious signs of alcohol abuse and alcoholism. They happen when you stop using alcohol. A hangover is a withdrawal symptom. Other late-stage withdrawal symptoms may include elevated blood pressure, pulse and breathing, mental confusion, disorientation, blackouts, tremors, seizures and delirium tremens (DTS) which can be fatal.

Increased craving for alcohol is another long-term effect of binge and problem drinking. It happens when you try to stop drinking or fend off withdrawal symptoms. Booze becomes an obsession that gets stronger and stronger and your life revolves around procuring and consuming it.

You have no control over your drinking when you're addicted to alcohol. You are unable to stop drinking once you start. And you become completely dependent on it - physically and psychologically.

Death is the ultimate long-term effect of binge drinking. It may be from one night of hard partying and you die from alcohol poisoning. Or it may be from alcohol-related health problems you develop that worsen over the years. No matter when or how it happens, booze is to blame.

Remember, these are just the physical effects of binge or problem drinking. They don't include the psychological, relationship, social, school, work, legal or financial problems caused by it.

Long-Term Physical Effects of Binge Drinking

- *You suffer from cell, tissue and organ damage*
- *You develop liver disease*
- *You develop pancreas disease*
- *You develop digestive system diseases*
- *You develop heart disease*
- *You suffer from brain damage*
- *You increase your risk of cancer*
- *You suffer from malnutrition*
- *You suffer from anemia*
- *You suffer from internal bleeding*
- *Your growth is stunted*
- *You develop a high tolerance to alcohol*
- *You suffer from withdrawal symptoms*
- *You develop an increased alcohol craving*
- *You have no control over drinking*
- *You develop a physical and psychological dependence on alcohol*
- *You die from alcohol poisoning or other alcohol-related health problems*

FYI - Know How to Handle Alcohol Poisoning and Asphyxiation!

What are the symptoms of alcohol poisoning? Mental confusion, stupor, coma, a passed out person who cannot be roused. The person's breathing may be slow - less than eight breaths per minute. Their breathing may be irregular - ten seconds or more between breaths. Their breathing may stop. Their heart beat may become slow or irregular. Their heart may stop. They may be suffering from hypothermia - low body temperature - and they may have a pale or bluish skin color. They may become severely dehydrated from vomiting and become hypoglycemic - suffering from low blood sugar - which can cause seizures, permanent brain damage or death. They can choke on their own vomit.

Don't wait for all of these symptoms to be present when deciding if a person is seriously ill or dying from alcohol poisoning. A person who is passed out and cannot be roused is seriously ill and may die. Also, know a person's blood alcohol concentration (BAC) can continue to rise even when he or she is passed out. Alcohol in the stomach and intestines continues to enter the bloodstream and circulates throughout the body even after they stop drinking. And keep in mind it's common for someone who drinks lots of alcohol to vomit, since alcohol is an irritant to the stomach. So there is a danger of choking on vomit, which can cause death by asphyxiation in a person who is not conscious. Finally, alcohol depresses nerves that control involuntary bodily functions, such as breathing. A fatal dose of alcohol will eventually stop these functions and the person will die. Be aware of these dangers.

What should you do for someone suffering alcohol poisoning? Don't wait, thinking the person will sleep it off. Don't try to guess the level of a person's drunkenness or their blood alcohol concentration (BAC). And don't be afraid to seek medical help for a friend. Don't worry if your friend gets angry or embarrassed. Be safe, not sorry. If there's any suspicion of an alcohol overdose, call 911 for help immediately. Even if a person survives extreme alcohol intoxication or poisoning, they can suffer from irreversible brain damage for the rest of their life.

<u>*Symptoms of Alcohol Poisoning*</u>

- *Mental confusion*
- *Stupor*
- *Coma*
- *A person who is passed out and cannot be roused*
- *Vomiting*
- *Seizures*
- *Stopped, slow or irregular breathing*
- *Stopped, slow or irregular heart beat*
- *Low body temperature*
- *Low blood sugar*
- *Pale or bluish skin color*
- *A person chokes on their vomit*
- *Death*

<u>*If a Person Suffers From Severe Alcohol Intoxication or Poisoning . . .*</u>

- *Call 911 Immediately!*

Teaser

Record all of the short-term and long-term physical and health problems you've had because of drinking. If you're suffering from any alcohol-related health problems, you should stop drinking immediately.

What's more important to you? Breath or the bottle?

Chapter Four:
What Other Ways Does Binge Drinking Affect You?

Now size up how alcohol affects other aspects of your life - psychological, behavioral, social, school, work, legal and financial. Could you improve the quality of your life if you drink smart?

Psychological Problems Caused by Drinking

Your self-esteem - your self-worth or what you think of yourself - is one of the first things to suffer if you've got a drinking problem. One or two drinks may lift your spirits and your self-esteem. But, simply put, the more you drink, the less you like yourself.

When you overdo it and get drunk, you say and do things you regret later. Or you black out and can't remember what happened when you were loaded. Or you get yourself in hot water for doing wild and crazy things. Whatever the case, you feel ashamed. You feel embarrassed. You feel guilty. You beat yourself up and these negative feelings eat away at you and your self-esteem.

You may also feel you have no control over your drinking. Or you drink until you're drunk. Or you feel uncomfortable if you go without booze. Drinking is becoming more and more important to you and you're worried about it. But in spite of these feelings, you continue to drink. You hate yourself for your drinking and these feelings continue to erode your self-esteem.

Your mood is the next thing to go if you binge or have a drinking problem. Sure, one or two beers may make you feel relaxed and happy most of the time. That's the upside. But if you're in a bad mood when you start drinking, too much alcohol will often accentuate that bad mood. If you're unhappy, frustrated, angry or irritable to begin with, expect to feel even worse after drinking. The drinking cure doesn't work in this case.

Heavy drinking also makes you more susceptible to mood swings. One minute you're upbeat and the next minute you're upset - because of too much liquor. One minute you're laughing and the next minute you're crying - because of too many beers. You're never really sure how you'll feel after too much alcohol and that's scary.

Binge or problem drinking can also cause or contribute to emotional disorders, like depression, anxiety, panic attacks, paranoia, violent or suicidal thoughts and mental confusion. Depression and anxiety, in particular, are often caused from too much booze. And even if they aren't caused by alcohol abuse, they certainly are exacerbated by it.

Binge or problem drinking can destroy your self-esteem and ruin your mood. And it's time to rethink your drinking if it has a negative impact on your attitude.

Psychological Problems Caused by Drinking

- *You suffer from low self-esteem*
- *Alcohol accentuates your negative feelings*
- *Alcohol causes or accentuates mood swings*
- *Alcohol causes or exacerbates emotional disorders*

Behavioral Problems Caused by Drinking

Your behavior also goes down hill when you overindulge. Too much alcohol loosens you and your inhibitions up, so you do and say things you'd never dream of doing or saying if you're sober. You behave impulsively - not thinking about the consequences of your actions. You think you're invincible and you're more likely to take risks and expose yourself and others to dangerous situations. You behave erratically and become a loose cannon. And people don't know how you'll react when you drink so they avoid you.

You may be a mean drunk and have violent outbursts. You may have unplanned, unprotected sex when you're high. You might get behind the wheel of a car when you're toasted. You may become verbally and physically aggressive and abusive when you tie one on. You might break the law and get arrested when you get wasted. You might have an accident and hurt or kill yourself when you drink too much. You might have an accident and hurt or kill someone else when you drink too much. And you're less likely to be interested in healthy activities. Your behavior centers on drinking and alcohol instead.

Obviously, booze can dictate your behavior. And most of the time - especially when you get smashed - it's not for the better. More good reasons to rethink your drinking.

Behavioral Problems Caused by Drinking

- *You become less inhibited*
- *You become more impulsive*
- *You feel invincible and take more risks*
- *You expose yourself and others to dangerous situations*
- *You behave erratically*
- *You may become mean and violent*
- *You may have unplanned, unprotected sex*
- *You may drink and drive*

- *You may become verbally and/or physically aggressive and/or abusive*
- *You may break the law and get arrested*
- *You may hurt or kill yourself*
- *You may hurt or kill others*
- *You lose interest in healthy activities*
- *Your behavior centers around drinking and alcohol*

Social Problems Caused by Drinking

No doubt about it, moderate drinking is a social lubricant and can pump up your self-confidence when you're partying. Just a drink or two though. More than that and liquor will backfire.

If you abuse alcohol, one of the first things you sacrifice is your reputation - what other people think of you. It's one of your most precious possessions, but if you drink too much, lose control, become loud, obnoxious or violent, you lose it. Worthwhile people don't want to hang out with you. You're an embarrassment to them. And they certainly don't want to do business with you - a person who can't hold their liquor. In most cases, it takes years to recover your reputation once it's been ruined by binge or problem drinking.

You suffer the stigma of a drinking problem too. When you drink heavily, you act irrationally and become less reliable and trustworthy. You'll do anything for a drink. People come to see you as an alcoholic, a lush, a barfly, a loser, a wino, the town drunk. It also takes years to live down the stigma of a drinking problem.

Your relationships suffer when you hit the bottle too. Excessive drinking alienates you from family, friends and colleagues. When you binge, you become less inhibited and you're more likely to argue and say and do things you regret. You may become estranged from your family because of your drinking. Some friends might want to cut ties with you because of it. Others might put up with it for a while, but lose patience and lose touch with you. Gradually, the only people left in your social circle are other problem drinkers.

Your family and friends may take you aside and talk to you about your drinking. They're worried about you. They've noticed how liquor is affecting you and the direction of your life and they speak up. Hopefully, you listen and take notice, instead of blowing up and blowing them off.

When you have a problem with alcohol you have less interest in family and friends. You don't invest time or energy in your relationships with them. They're just not that important to you anymore. Your relationship with booze is more important to you than your relationships with people.

Eventually, drinking alone becomes your favorite pastime. You've alienated family and friends - even some problem drinking pals. Alcohol is your best friend and your only form of entertainment. If you're not careful, you could end up alone because of booze.

Social Problems Caused by Drinking

- *You ruin your reputation*
- *You suffer the stigma of a drinking problem*
- *You alienate your family and friends*
- *Your family and friends talk to you about your drinking*
- *You don't invest time or energy in relationships*
- *Relationships are no longer important to you*
- *You drink alone*
- *Alcohol becomes your best friend and only entertainment*

School Problems Caused by Drinking

Research shows you're more likely to miss class and spend less time studying, if you binge or have a drinking problem. You're also more likely to get behind in school work and have lower grades, than students who don't binge. And if you keep drinking heavily, there's a good chance you'll flunk out and never graduate.

If you don't graduate from high school or get your college diploma because of alcohol abuse, your future will not look bright. You'll feel bad about your underachieving self, you won't make the money you want to make, you won't be able to afford things or activities you're interested in, your lifestyle will suffer and life will be harder in general - because of problem drinking.

You could suffer for the rest of your life if you don't complete your education because of abuse alcohol. Simply put, you won't live up to your full potential.

School Problems Caused by Drinking

- *You miss class often*
- *You spend less time studying*
- *You get behind in school work*
- *You get lower grades*
- *You don't graduate*
- *You don't live up to your full potential*

Work Problems Caused by Drinking

You show up late to work because of too much partying the night before. Or you show up, but you're so hung over you don't get a thing done. Or you don't show up at all and take a sick day. Your reputation is shot. You never get promoted. You never get a raise. And you get fired.

Binge or problem drinking have led to many a layoff. Who wants a person who hits the bottle working for them? They're not productive, reliable or trustworthy. They love liquor more than they love their job or their paycheck.

If you're a boozer, you'll probably end up working a string of low paying jobs that go nowhere. After one or two years you'll leave or you'll get fired because of your drinking problem. Drinking does not impress the boss.

<u>Work Problems Caused by Drinking</u>

- *You're late often*
- *You're hung over and not productive at work*
- *You take more sick days*
- *You're not reliable or trustworthy*
- *You never get a promotion*
- *You never get a raise*
- *You get fired*
- *You hold a string of low paying jobs and never get ahead*

Legal Problems Caused by Drinking

Getting drunk is a formal invitation to a jail cell. Drinking and driving, being intoxicated in public, damaging property, having accidents or getting into fights when you're under the influence guarantees a brush with the law sooner or later.

If you hurt or kill someone when you're drinking and you're convicted of assault and battery, vehicular manslaughter or homicide, you can kiss your life goodbye. You'll be an ex-con when you get out of prison - after you've paid your debt to society.

Getting ticketed or arrested for drunk driving - even if you don't hurt someone - is also serious business and costs - legally, financially, socially and psychologically. You'll have a DUI or DWI on your record, you'll fork over thousands for court fines, lawyer's fees, drunk driving school fees and increased insurance premiums. You may be ordered to rehab or have to wear an alcohol-monitoring device and your driver's license may be restricted, suspended or revoked causing you great inconvenience - you'll be stuck at home wondering how to get to school or work. You don't want to drink and drive!

BTW, you don't have to be legally drunk - registering a .08 BAC or higher - to have problems with the law. Police can also ticket you for being "under the influence" - being high on booze, but not registering a .08 BAC.

Getting a fake ID can also get you arrested. So can trying to buy liquor if you're underage. So can getting someone else to buy it for you if you're underage. Anyway you look at it, underage drinking, a fake ID, trying to buy booze if you're under twenty-one or having someone else buy it for you will eventually land you in hot water.

Just one arrest when you're high can decimate your bank account, freedom, happiness and future. Life is hard enough - without having legal problems caused by alcohol abuse.

<u>Legal Problems Caused by Drinking</u>

- *You get arrested for public drunkenness, assault and battery, vandalism, vehicular manslaughter, homicide, etc.*
- *You get ticketed or arrested for drunk driving or driving under the influence*
- *Your driver's license is restricted, suspended or revoked*
- *You go to jail*
- *You fight lawsuits*
- *You have an arrest record*

Financial Problems Caused by Drinking

Lawyer's fees and court fines might break you if you get arrested for alcohol-related legal offenses. If you're charged with drunk driving in California, most first time DUI offenders are charged with a misdemeanor and may be arrested, which can add up to thousands of dollars. Bail is usually set at $500. Car towing and storage can run up to $1,000. Lawyer's fees can cost up to $5,000, but that doesn't include the hourly rate they charge if you go to trial. Court fines can run up to $2,500. DUI classes for first-time offenders cost between $500 and $1,000, but repeat offenders pay about $1,600. And your insurance premium will skyrocket for years after the arrest.

If you're a repeat offender, you may also lose your license and/or serve time in jail. You'll miss school, work and income. You'll have to figure out alternative transportation. You will be greatly inconvenienced in many different ways. Yes, getting arrested because of booze can be expensive in more ways than one.

If you hurt yourself or someone else when you're drinking, you'll be looking at even more bills. If you injure yourself, you'll have medical bills and may have to take time off from work. If you injure someone else, you'll be paying their medical bills, fighting costly lawsuits and paying out settlements. These legal problems could go on for years and bankrupt you.

The money you save for something special - for school, a car, a house or a trip - will be eaten up by legal fees and settlements. Your savings will be depleted because of your actions while you were under the influence. You'll be broke.

Your money and your future will be up in smoke if you let liquor take over. Think about it.

Financial Problems Caused by Drinking

- *You pay court fines*
- *You pay lawyer's fees*
- *You pay to go to drunk driving school*
- *You pay to go to rehab*
- *You pay higher insurance premiums*
- *You miss work*
- *You pay medical bills*
- *You pay off lawsuits*
- *Your savings are depleted*
- *You're broke*

Teaser

What psychological, behavioral, social, school, work, legal or financial problems have binge or problem drinking caused in your life? Record them. They might just motivate you to drink smart, not dumb, if you're going to drink.

Chapter Five:
How Do You Measure Up?

If you have any health, psychological, social, school, work, financial or legal problems because of alcohol, you're a problem drinker. And, more specifically, if you're a guy who has had five or more drinks in a row over a two hour period or a girl who has had four or more drinks in a row over a two hour period, you're a binge drinker. Remember - there are many different forms of problem drinking and binge drinking is just one form of alcohol abuse.

Be honest with yourself. Own up to a drinking problem - even if you rarely get drunk. Then do something about it - before it messes up your big, beautiful life!

How Does Drinking Currently Affect Your Life?

Do you get drunk? Do you have blackouts? How about hangovers? Any health problems caused by excessive alcohol consumption? Any stomach or digestive problems, headaches or sleeping problems because of drinking? If you get wasted or have blackouts, hangovers or health challenges caused by booze, you've got a drinking problem.

How about psychological problems. Do you suffer from low self-esteem - you don't feel good about yourself - because of how much and how often you drink? Do you experience emotional highs and lows and mood swings triggered because of alcohol? Are you quick to anger or do you have temper tantrums when you're high? Do you feel stressed, depressed, anxious or fearful because of booze? Is liquor keeping you from healthy activities, like sports or hobbies? All red flags you have a drinking problem.

How about relationship and social problems. Do you fight with family or friends when you drink or because you drink? Have family or friends talked to you about your drinking? Have they asked you to stop or cut down? Is alcohol keeping you from social events and activities? Would you rather drink than socialize? More red flags.

What about school and work problems. Is partying to blame for cutting class or not studying? For flunking out or not graduating? Does drinking make you late for work or take sick days? Has your boss ever taken you aside and told you to lighten up on the liquor? Have you ever been fired because of your alcohol use? Do you drag yourself through the day at school or work because you're hung over? Even more red flags.

What about money and legal problems. Is beer taking a bite out of your budget? Are you having a hard time holding down a job and paying your bills because of too much partying? Do you spend more money on liquor than food? Do you have any alcohol-related legal problems - DUI's or DWI's, accidents, getting arrested for public drunkenness, picking fights or damaging property while you were under the influence? Red flags are flying.

If you're suffering from any of these alcohol abuse symptoms, you're a problem drinker. And if you're a guy who downs five or more drinks over a two hour period or a girl who downs four or more drinks over a two hour period, you're a binge drinker. Don't deny it, minimize it or distort it. Be straight with yourself. You can't fix what you don't acknowledge!

How Has Drinking Affected You in the Past?

Having trouble deciding if you need help with alcohol? Try looking at your drinking habits over the last three months. How many times did you get drunk? How many times did you have a hangover? How many times did you have a blackout? Ever feel ashamed of your behavior when you were high? Has your drinking caused problems with family, friends, colleagues or strangers? Has your drinking kept you from fulfilling important obligations, like going to school or work? Any legal or money problems because of alcohol use?

If you can say yes to any one of these questions, you're a problem drinker. And if you're a guy who consumes five or more drinks over a two hour period or a girl who consumes four or more drinks over a two hour period, you're a binge drinker.

Start a Drinking Diary

Still unable to decide if you're a binge or problem drinker? Start a drinking diary. Every time you drink, record how much you drink, how long you drink and any negative consequences associated with your alcohol use - getting drunk, having blackouts or hangovers, reduced study time, fighting with family or friends, being late for work, etc. Keep this diary for at least three months or until you have a problem drinking episode.

If, after three months, you haven't experienced a single symptom of alcohol abuse, you don't have a problem with liquor. But if, after three months, you notice any health, psychological, social, school, work, legal or financial problems caused by booze, you're a problem drinker. And if you're a guy whose had five or more drinks in a row over a two hour period or a girl whose had four or more drinks in a row over a two hour period - you're a binge drinker specifically.

Get started on your drinking diary today if you're still questioning what kind of drinker you are.

Still Unable to Decide If You Binge?

If you're still not sure if you're a binge drinker or a problem drinker - after reviewing your current and past drinking habits and keeping a drinking diary - you need professional help. Talk to your school counselor, a psychologist, your physician or clergyman. Maybe they can shed some light on the situation and you'll know what the score is.

Teaser

What problems in your life are directly or indirectly related to your drinking? Record them. Are you a problem drinker? Are you a binge drinker?

Part II:
To Drink Or
Not To Drink?

Chapter Six:
Why Do You Binge?

There could be so many reasons behind your drinking, where do you start? Here! Learn about the personal, environmental and biological factors that may drive you to drink, because the more you're aware of them, the less susceptible you'll be to them.

Personal Factors That May Drive You to Drink

You Drink to Get High and Have Fun

You probably want to drink alcohol for the same reasons most people want to drink alcohol: to get high and have fun. No rocket science here.

You're probably looking for a quick fix too. And beer delivers. You forget about the ups and downs of your day and start enjoying yourself within minutes.

Alcohol abuse happens when you lean on booze too much and too often to feel good. When liquor becomes your only source of fun, relaxation and entertainment, it becomes a problem - a drinking problem.

You Drink Because You're Curious

When you're young, you're curious and into new adventures. And that includes drinking adventures. You've been exposed to so many different messages about drinking and alcohol, now you want to try it and see for yourself.

Just keep your head and proceed with caution. You don't have to dive in, go off the deep end and get drunk if you drink. You might drown. If you choose to drink, just get your toes wet and see how a little liquor affects you before you dive head first into that beer bottle.

You Drink Because You're Into a Partying Lifestyle

If you adopt a partying lifestyle that centers on alcohol and socializing, you significantly increase your chances of developing a serious drinking problem. It's just common sense that the more you expose yourself to booze and equate drinking with socializing, the more you'll drink and the more you'll depend on liquor to have fun.

What kind of lifestyle do you lead? One that revolves around alcohol and partying? Or one that revolves around healthy living, friends, family, school, work and good, clean fun?

You Drink Because You've Been Told Good Things About Alcohol

Research shows if you've been taught that alcohol is fun and you can expect to have a good time when you're high, you're more likely to start drinking earlier, to drink more often and to drink more in general. Studies also show positive beliefs and expectations about spirits and its effects are established early in life. Before you were nine, you probably viewed alcohol in a negative way and saw drinking as bad. But by about age thirteen, your view of alcohol and its effects became more positive.

Positive beliefs about liquor you've picked up from family and friends play a huge role in your drinking behavior. Beliefs like thinking you're smarter and sexier when you're toasted. Or you're cool and make friends more easily if you join the drinking party. You may not even be aware of your positive beliefs about booze, but they trigger your drinking anyway.

Positive expectations about alcohol can also influence your drinking habits. If your parents expected to have fun when under the influence, you expect to have fun when under the influence. If your friends expect to be happy and relaxed when partying, you expect to be happy and relaxed when partying.

What are your positive beliefs about alcohol? What are your positive expectations about it? How have they affected your drinking behavior?

You Drink to Cope with Stress and Frustration

Do you aspire to be perfect? Or just pretty good? Do you go all out to be the best-looking, smartest, most popular, most athletic and most well-rounded person at your school or in your crowd? Do you want to get into a prestigious college? Or are you shooting for your dream job? Competition is fierce among young people these days and you're probably paying the price for perfection by feeling stressed and frustrated.

To make matters worse, you're also establishing your new adult identity, making your way in the world and planning your future - just a few of the challenges you're facing when transitioning from adolescence to adulthood. You're assuming more responsibilities, weighing school and career options, forming serious relationships, learning about sex, living on your own and managing money. You may be coping with family and financial problems too. Not to mention the physical changes happening in your body caused by surging hormones. You've got a lot going on. And the stress and frustration you must feel from tackling these enormous challenges may drive you to drink.

Other concerns may be making you crazy too. Peer pressure - how to fit in, what others think of you and who to hang out with. And you're also overbooked. You've been taught from an early age to have your days filled with productive activities. So when you're not studying to get straight A's, you're running from dance lessons to tennis lessons to science fairs to softball games. There isn't enough time in the day to get everything done you want to get done - which just adds to your stress load.

You're over stimulated too. Cell phones, texting, pagers, ipods, blackberries, PCs, internet, email, etc. You never have an unplugged moment to yourself to chill out and settle down. Your everyday life is a rush from one activity to another, fitting in as much as you can while you're talking on your cell, texting, emailing, learning or entertaining yourself with some computer game. You're overbooked and over stimulated. You've got your hands full. Full of stress and frustration that is.

What stresses you and triggers your drinking? What frustrates you and triggers your drinking?

You Drink to Boost Your Self-Esteem and Self-Confidence

Don't feel good about yourself? Are you constantly comparing yourself to others and putting yourself down? You have self-esteem issues. And when you don't think you're the greatest, you're more likely to turn to liquor to feel better and boost your confidence.

Too fat? Too skinny? Too dumb? Too smart? Bad skin? Bad grades? Clumsy? Dorky? Geeky? If you think of yourself in these terms, give it up. This negative thinking will make you even more unhappy and less self-assured.

The truth is, the more you like yourself, the more confident you feel and the less desire you have for alcohol and drugs. If you like yourself and feel sure of yourself, who needs beer?

Do you think your self-esteem and self-confidence - or lack of them - play a part in your drinking behavior?

You Drink to Cope with Psychological Problems and Emotions

If you feel depressed, anxious, withdrawn, angry or lonely or are prone to bad moods, you're more likely to start drinking at a younger age. Research also shows if you drink to cope with negative feelings, the more likely you'll engage in heavy drinking and have problems with alcohol.

What makes you depressed? Looks, grades, relationships, money? You're also entering the adult world and you're expected to make your own way now. That means increased responsibilities. Maybe facing the world on your own and assuming more responsibility is bringing you down.

What makes you anxious? Afraid you won't be able to make the grade in college or at work? Afraid you won't have enough money to go to school or pay your bills? Worried your girlfriend or boyfriend is going to dump you? Afraid of failure? Afraid of success? Worried about your future? Whatever you're afraid of may be making you anxious.

What makes you withdrawn, angry, lonely or prone to bad moods? Changing relationships? You're more independent and your parents are letting go. And close friends may also be on the move. You rarely see them and you grow apart. Plus, you don't know a soul at your new school or at work. The ups and downs of a romantic relationship? Having a girlfriend or boyfriend is a learning experience and doesn't always work out. Sex? Sexual identity? Money? You name it. Many different issues could trigger your negative feelings and moods. Identify them and deal with them.

Do feelings factor into your drinking? Do you medicate with alcohol?

You Drink Because You Have Certain Personality Characteristics That Lead to Risky Behavior

Certain personality traits - like being impulsive, risk-taking, non-conforming, rebellious, anti-social, hyperactive, aggressive, feeling invincible and invulnerable and always seeking exciting new experiences - have all been linked to drinking more alcohol, more often.

Maybe you think booze in and of itself is an exciting new adventure. Or that it will open the door to exciting new adventures. Or that drinking is a good way to express your freedom and individuality. Maybe you think bingeing is a great way to rebel - poking society and all of its rules in the eye. You may think you're invincible and you'll never have a problem with beer, so you drink as much as you can. Or that guzzling is a harmless way to kill time or settle yourself down when you feel hyper. Maybe you drink to cope with pent-up anger and aggression you know is unacceptable when you're sober.

Sure, most of us have experienced these adolescent personality traits at times. But when taken to the extreme, they could be hazardous to your health. These thoughts and attitudes may rationalize binge drinking which could lead to alcohol poisoning, drunk driving and accidents. You do want to survive adolescence and young adulthood, don't you?

What personality characteristics can you identify with? Which ones influence your drinking?

Personal Factors That May Drive You to Drink

- *You drink to get high and have fun*
- *You drink because you're curious*
- *You drink because you're into a partying lifestyle*
- *You drink because you've been told good things about alcohol*
- *You drink to cope with stress and frustration*
- *You drink to boost your self-esteem and self-confidence*
- *You drink to cope with psychological problems and emotions*
- *You drink because you have certain personality characteristics that lead to risky behavior*

Environmental Factors That May Drive You to Drink

You Drink Because You Live in An Alcohol-Saturated Culture

No wonder you're interested in booze. It's probably your drug of choice because it's legal, cheap, convenient, socially acceptable, it works fast and feels good. And you're constantly bombarded with positive messages about it everywhere - at home, at friend's homes, at your fraternity or sorority, on TV, radio, billboards, the internet, at sporting events, concerts, parties, social events, convenience stores, on campus and around the corner at the local pizza parlor or tavern. You can't escape it. To make matters worse, research shows young people are more susceptible to advertising - including alcohol advertising - than adults.

At home, wine, beer or spirits might be kept in the fridge right next to the milk and eggs. Your parents and their friends may drink - socially without problems or abusively with problems - sending you the message that alcohol is okay.

Some of your friends may have started talking about drinking or actually started drinking when they were ten, eleven or twelve. Some may have started bingeing and getting drunk when they were in elementary school. Maybe you were tempted to join in and did.

Alcohol probably became a more serious subject for you in high school. Perhaps your drinking became or is becoming more frequent - especially on the weekends. And friends may be pressuring you to drink and get drunk with them, even though you might not want to. You feel the pressure to fit in and to many young people, drinking beer is the way to do it. You may also use alcohol to make a statement to yourself and society. You're growing up, breaking away and becoming an adult. You're declaring your independence with liquor and becoming your own person by drinking. At least you think so.

When you reach college, boozing starts your very first week of higher education. Besides, it takes the edge off of the stress you feel adjusting to college life - living on your own for the first time, meeting new people, making new friends and facing a tough course load. A beer sounds good on Friday night.

In fact, college is drunk on beer and alcohol is everywhere. All sporting events - football, baseball, basketball and soccer games. At fraternity and sorority parties and during hazing. Special events, like homecoming and spring break, and not-so-special events, like pub crawls and toga and keg parties, all include drinking and getting drunk. You're often exposed to drinking games, including beer pong and jello shots. Beer and wine might even be served on campus - at the cafeteria or student union. There are beer bars all around campus catering to you and your college budget too. No matter where you look or what kind of entertainment you're into, spirits are always in the picture.

Even if you don't go to college, liquor is aggressively marketed to you - and you may not even be aware of it. Alcohol companies spend five billion dollars a year selling booze to you through traditional advertising and by sponsoring many major league baseball, football, basketball and soccer teams and professional sporting events, including the super bowl, the World Series and March madness. They also sponsor concerts and major music acts and establish associations with professional athletes, celebrities and supermodels to push their products. And they've developed "education programs" for teens, young adults and parents which superficially discourage drinking, but really promote it. The alcohol industry has shaped your beliefs and attitudes about liquor, whether you know it or not.

What messages about alcohol have you been exposed to today? This week? Recognize them, then dismiss them.

You Drink Because of Family Influences

Even though genes may play a role in your drinking, they don't tell the whole story. Drinking behavior is actually the result of a complex interaction between heredity and environmental factors. And environmental factors at home can have a huge impact on your drinking behavior and attitudes.

Your parent's alcohol use can affect your drinking in three different ways. First, they set an example for you with their own drinking habits. You learn when to drink, what to drink, how to drink, how much to drink and how often to drink from your parents. For example, if your parents are moderate social drinkers, the more likely you'll pick up their moderate drinking habits. But if they're problem drinkers, the more likely you'll pick up their problem drinking habits.

Second, you learn and internalize your parent's beliefs and expectations about alcohol as you're growing up. If liquor is only for celebrations or special occasions, you learn that booze is only for certain events. If it's used everyday to cope with stress, you learn that drinking is a daily stress-reducing activity. If your parents are careless drinkers and they get drunk every time they party, you learn that getting smashed every time you socialize is normal.

The quality of your relationship with your parents is the third way they can affect your drinking behavior. A good or bad relationship with them can be linked to alcohol use or abuse. The better your relationship is, the less you'll be drawn to booze to rebel or improve your mood. The worse your relationship is, the more you'll be drawn to booze to rebel or improve your mood.

Your parent's drinking example can influence your alcohol habits for the rest of your life. Think about your drinking pattern - when, where, why, how often and how much you drink. Is your pattern similar to your parents? Then think about your beliefs and expectations about liquor. Are they similar to your parents? Finally, what kind of relationship do you have with your parents? Do you use alcohol as a weapon to get back at them or to make yourself feel better or both? Or do you all get along - without booze in the picture? If you know where you picked up your drinking habits, you can control them and your drinking.

You Drink Because of Peer Pressure and Approval

Peer pressure and social acceptance are common reasons for young people to drink and binge. You want to be liked and popular, so you drink to fit in. You want to create new friendships and deepen existing ones at school or work, so you party. You want to be more important in your friend's eyes, so you drink everyone else under the table. There are so many good reasons to get wasted when you're in the company of others!

Do peer pressure and social acceptance trip your drinking and bingeing? Think about your reasons for drinking when you party.

You Drink Because You Reside in a Fraternity or Sorority

It's sad but true. If you live in a fraternity or sorority house, you're more likely to be exposed to alcohol more often, you're more likely to engage in drinking games and you're more likely to binge.

For many fraternities and sororities the emphasis is on socializing and getting smashed - not on studying. You major in beer, not math, and if you're not careful you'll leave college with a drinking problem - not a diploma.

If you're considering joining a fraternity or sorority, what's the emphasis on partying and booze? If beer is the main event, you may want to reconsider.

You Drink Because of Your Marital, Family and Career Status

If you're single, you probably drink more than if you're married. Committing to marriage means you're assuming adult roles and responsibilities and you drink less because of the limitations that these roles and responsibilities place on you and your social activities. Young married women have the greatest decrease in alcohol consumption and married men have the fewest increases. But divorce leads to increased drinking for both men and women.

And becoming a parent is linked to lower alcohol use for both men and women. You increase your workload and obligations with children which curbs your intake.

If you work full-time after high school, instead of going on to college, you may experience a slight increase in your alcohol consumption. If you're a young person who has joined the military, you may tend to drink heavily - five or more drinks per drinking occasion at least once a week - compared to older enlistees who drink less. And if you're an unemployed man, you probably drink less than an unemployed woman.

Interesting facts. How does your marital, family and career status affect your drinking?

Environmental Factors That May Drive You to Drink

- *You drink because you live in an alcohol-saturated culture*
- *You drink because of family influences*
- *You drink because of peer pressure and approval*
- *You drink because you reside in a fraternity or sorority*
- *You drink because of your marital, family and career status*

Biological Factors That May Drive You to Drink

You Drink Because Your Brain Is Not Fully Developed

Did you know your brain keeps developing into your twenties? And it's this long developmental period that could explain some thinking and behavior in young people - like impulsive, thrill-seeking behavior and not thinking about the consequences of their actions - that leads them to seek out new and potentially dangerous experiences, like trying alcohol and drugs?

Your brain is not yet fully developed, so you push the envelope with alcohol. But don't blame all of your antics on your poor, underdeveloped brain. You do have some say in the matter!

You Drink Because of Genes and Heredity

Does alcohol abuse or alcoholism run in your family? If it does, you may have a genetic predisposition for drinking problems, including a high tolerance for alcohol which may be inherited.

It's a fact that if one of your parents is an alcoholic or if you have several family members who are alcoholics, you have a greater risk of developing alcoholism. Research shows if you're the child of an alcoholic, you are between four and ten times more likely to become an alcoholic, compared to a child who has no close relatives who are alcoholics. You're also more likely to start drinking at a younger age and develop a drinking problem early on. People with a family history of alcoholism are also less likely to grow out of a drinking problem, compared to people with no family history of it.

Are there alcohol abusers in your family? If alcoholism runs in your family, you have to be extra vigilant about booze.

You Drink More Because You Have a Higher Tolerance to Alcohol

Some young people have a higher tolerance to alcohol than others, so when they drink, they drink in excess to achieve the desired effect. Studies have also shown some young drinkers can consume a lot more liquor than adults before suffering from negative consequences, like having hangovers or blackouts. This very high tolerance to alcohol may explain why some young drinkers binge.

Do you have a high tolerance to alcohol? Do you drink more than your friends to achieve the desired effect?

You Drink More Because You're More Sensitive to the Positive Effects of Alcohol

Some young people seem to be more sensitive to the positive effects of alcohol than others. And these positive effects, like feeling relaxed and comfortable in social settings, reinforce drinking and getting drunk.

Are you super sensitive to the positive effects of alcohol? Do you think this sensitivity factors into your drinking behavior?

You Drink Because of Gender, Race, Ethnicity and Cultural Factors

Gender may play a role in your drinking. Men are more likely to drink in harmful ways than women. A recent national survey of nineteen to thirty year-olds showed forty-five percent of men and almost twenty-seven percent of women reported heavy drinking - five or more drinks on one occasion in the past two weeks. And a little over seven percent of the men and three percent of the women reported daily drinking.

Racial, ethnic and cultural differences may also affect your drinking habits and attitudes. In general, White and Native American young adults drink more than African Americans and Asians and drinking rates for Hispanics fall in the middle. Drinking peaks for Whites between the ages of nineteen and twenty-two, while heavy drinking among African Americans and Hispanics peaks later and persists longer into adulthood.

Biological Factors That May Drive You to Drink

- *You drink because your brain is not fully developed*
- *You drink because of genes and heredity*
- *You drink more because you have a higher tolerance to alcohol*
- *You drink more because you're more sensitive to the positive effects of alcohol*
- *You drink because of gender, race, ethnicity and cultural factors*

Teaser

Make a list of all the personal, environmental and biological factors that may drive you to drink or binge. The more you know, the less you'll drink!

Chapter Seven:
Twenty-One Great Reasons
Not to Binge

Here are some terrific reasons to drink smart, not dumb. Think about them - especially when you're thinking of drinking.

1. Binge Drinking Prevents You From Living Life to the Fullest

Drinking too much and too often will make getting the most out of life nearly impossible. If you want to graduate from college, surf in Hawaii, make a movie, own your own business, become a parent, climb Mt. Everest, become a millionaire, write a novel, start a band or help others, bingeing won't get you there.

You simply wouldn't have the time or the energy you need to make your life happen. You'd be too busy drinking or recovering from the effects of drinking. How could you possibly achieve your lofty goals if you abused alcohol? You couldn't.

What do you want out of life? What would you like to accomplish in the next ten or twenty years? Where does alcohol fit in?

2. You Have a Natural Ability to Have Fun Without Alcohol

You're young, fit and at the top of your game - physically and mentally. You're brimming with energy, enthusiasm and creativity. And, hopefully, you know you can have fun and celebrate life without any mind-altering substances - including beer.

Natural highs, without booze, are the best. You'll remember them for the rest of your life, compared to drug or alcohol-induced highs which you'll forget over time.

Another benefit of a natural high? Just knowing you can feel good without drugs or alcohol boosts your self-esteem and self-confidence. You like yourself more and you're more self-assured when you know you don't have to rely on a substance to be happy and meet the challenges in life.

Yes - you have a natural ability to have fun without beer. No - you don't have to binge, get drunk, blackout, vomit, pass out, be hung over or suffer from alcohol poisoning to enjoy yourself.

3. You'll Enhance Your Reputation If You Control Alcohol

Even though you think you don't care about what other people think of you, you do. Your good reputation is important to you - even when you're drinking. Sure, some friends and acquaintances will encourage you to drink and get drunk to fit in. And you may think you have to drink to feel like one of the crowd on occasion. But the truth is most young people disapprove of friends who drink in excess and think less of them.

The bottom line is that when you act smart, independent and in control around alcohol, you'll enhance your reputation. You'll earn other people's respect and admiration when you drink moderately. And they'll see you as a stand-up person.

Do you want to be known as a loser who can't hold their liquor? To be known as a crazy who goes berserk when they're under the influence? To be known as a mean drunk when they've had too much beer? You don't. You want to be known as someone who controls alcohol and is not controlled by it. An intelligent, reliable person who isn't a slave to a substance or an addiction. It's your choice and your reputation.

4. You'll Accent Your Individuality, Independence and Intelligence If You Don't Binge

You're your own person. You're smart and independent and you don't necessarily go along with the crowd, if what the crowd is doing doesn't work for you. You're not a follower, but a free-thinking individual determined to set your own course in life. You're not going to be pressured into anything - including drinking - by others. And controlling your drinking, not bingeing or abusing alcohol, is a great way for you to express your individuality, independence and intelligence.

When was the last time you bucked the crowd and went your own way? When everyone else was dyeing their hair blue, were you dyeing yours orange? When everyone else was getting tattoos, were you having your tats removed? When everyone else was bingeing and getting drunk, were you in control?

Think about the times you expressed your individuality, independence and intelligence and didn't go with the flow. You felt powerful when you followed your inner voice. Listen to your wise inner voice in drinking situations too. Then show people who's the boss when it comes to booze. You are.

5. You'll Be Happier and Like Yourself More If You Don't Binge

The less you drink, the less likely you'll say and do things that will make you unhappy. You won't make yourself sick on alcohol and have hangovers, you won't have fights with friends and family about your drinking, you won't drink and drive, you won't do something stupid that will harm yourself or others, you won't get arrested and you won't ruin your reputation or your future - if you keep liquor in check. In other words, you'll avoid a lot of problems if you avoid binge drinking.

Just think of how happy you could be if you never had to deal with the consequences of bingeing again. No alcohol-related problems eating away at you, your self-esteem or your life. Food for thought.

6. You're More Likely to Get Good Grades and Graduate If You Don't Binge

Research shows the more you drink, the more you miss class, the less you study, the more you get behind in school and the lower your grade point average is. You're less likely to graduate too.

Think of all the time you'd have on your hands if you cut out binge or problem drinking. Everything you needed to get done would get done. You'd make class more often, you'd keep up with your studies, you'd get better grades and you'd graduate. And you'd be more successful in life if you graduated.

Your future hinges on your education, whether you like it or not. And alcohol and education don't mix. Just the facts, so you can make informed drinking decisions.

7. You'll Enjoy Peace of Mind Not Worrying About Alcohol Abuse

Peace of mind. Total tranquility. Taking all of the pain, shame and heartache that go with a drinking problem off the table, so you'd never worry about it again. What a relief - especially if alcoholism runs in your family.

Peace of mind can be yours if you eliminated binge or problem drinking. It's worth it.

8. You Could Die From Binge Drinking

We're talking about you dying from alcohol poisoning, being killed in a drunk driving accident or doing something stupid when you're drunk that would mortally injure you - like jumping off buildings, starting fires or drowning.

You have your whole life ahead of you - if you survive binge drinking. Dying young from an alcohol-related accident would be the ultimate price to pay for just one night of bingeing. Is it worth it?

9. Binge Drinking Could Alter the Course of Your Life

Hurting yourself, hurting or killing someone else, getting pregnant, getting arrested, getting sued, going into debt to pay off medical bills, legal fees and settlements, getting fired from your job, getting kicked out of school, becoming estranged from your family and friends and losing your driver's license are also high prices to pay for one night of bingeing.

Just one of these events could alter the course of your life forever. Imagine what a mess your life could be if you kept hitting the bottle.

10. Binge Drinking Could Step On Your Good Time

Brainstorm all of the exciting things you'd like to do. Personal and professional goals and fun, entertaining pursuits, destinations or things. Traveling around the world? Buying a Ferrari? Going skiing, hiking, camping, mountain climbing or trekking? Joining the Peace Corp? Planting a vineyard? Getting a PhD? Running marathons? Living in Italy? Making music? Making a movie? Riding a Harley? Raising a child? Going on a safari? Running your own business?

Could you make your dreams happen if you drank heavily? Probably not. And even if you did get around to them, you probably wouldn't do them very well or enjoy them very much. If you drank too much, too often, you wouldn't have the energy, coordination or commitment to follow through with your goals, especially ones that required any intellectual or athletic ability. You'd be physically and mentally impaired from alcohol and hung over most of the time - not fit for anything.

When you're forty or fifty years old, do you want any regrets? Regrets about things you didn't get around to because you were too busy drinking or recovering from drinking? You don't.

11. Binge Drinking Prevents You From Having Good Friends and Relationships

If the crowd you hang out with thinks it's cool to binge, chances are your pals aren't good friend material. They're superficial and their values are out of whack. They probably value alcohol and getting drunk more than they value you. Not exactly a solid foundation to build healthy relationships on.

If you choose to drink moderately, on the other hand, you will be attracted to a better quality of people and a better quality of people will be attracted to you. Worthwhile people who respect you and your accomplishments, not how much beer you can down in one sitting. These people are not only better relationship material, they're more interesting too. Most likely, they have a lot going on and are focused on achieving their goals and living well. They're not numbing out on booze all night and recovering from hangovers all day.

Who do you want to get tight with? People who value you for you or people who look up to you because of your alcohol consumption?

12. Binge Drinking Stunts Your Growth

Alcohol affects every cell in your young body and it can actually stunt your growth. If you drink heavily when you're young, booze will prevent you from developing physically and can permanently damage your body. You could also develop lifelong health problems at an early age.

Liquor is not harmless, even though it's legal, convenient and socially acceptable. It's toxic and you could suffer for the rest of your life if you binge when you're young.

13. Binge Drinking Stunts Your Neurological Development

Your brain continues to develop throughout adolescence and young adulthood and scientists think that drinking alcohol during this time may lead to serious problems in brain functioning. In fact, young drinkers can permanently damage their memory and the parts of their brain where learning, critical thinking and the ability to make sound decisions take place. Heavy drinking can also impair coordination and motor skills. Researchers think if you binge on a regular basis, you suffer from alcohol withdrawal after these binges, which causes these neurological problems.

To make matters worse, adolescents need only drink half as much as adults to suffer negative neurological effects. Plus, they can't catch up with nondrinkers in brain development in adulthood. More great reasons to rethink binge drinking, if you choose to drink.

14. Binge Drinking Stunts Your Psychological Development

Bingeing when you're young could harm you psychologically too. It could undermine your self-esteem and self-confidence - two important qualities you need to be a happy, well-adjusted adult. And it could interfere with your psychological development. If you learn to rely on liquor when you're making the difficult transition from adolescence to adulthood, you might learn to rely on it whenever you hit a rough patch in life. Instead of dealing with life's challenges head on, you turn inward and to the bottle. Your psychological development is arrested before you grow up and you learn to depend on alcohol to cope.

Do you want to be stuck in adolescence for the rest of your life? You don't!

15. Binge Drinking Stunts Your Social Development

Drinking in excess can also harm you socially. You're about to become an adult with a whole new world opening up to you. A world which includes sex and adult relationships. And leaning on alcohol during this passage could prevent you from forming healthy relationships and developing socially.

Booze causes problems communicating with others - making meaningful relationships difficult. Drinking can also prevent you from dealing with and working through changing relationships. When a relationship gets rocky, you head for the bar, instead of working it out. The result is you never really enjoy healthy relationships or thrive socially.

You don't need alcohol as a crutch to get through life. You can have great relationships and be socially adept without it!

16. Binge Drinking Leads to Sexual Problems

Too much liquor can actually lower testosterone levels, the hormone that regulates the male sex drive. It can also lower sperm count and shrink testes in men. Binge drinking can make men impotent.

For women, alcohol in small doses may increase their sex drive like men, but in large doses it decreases their ability to have an orgasm. Many young women who abuse alcohol stop menstruating and may become infertile. And women who get drunk are more likely to become victims of date rape.

Both men and women are at greater risk for having sex when they're intoxicated. They're also less likely to use protection and get pregnant and more likely to get sexually-transmitted diseases.

How can you improve your sex life? Don't drink so much!

17. Binge Drinking Leads to a Life of Alcoholism

Careful. Most people establish alcohol use or abuse patterns in young adulthood. And research shows if you binge in your teen or college years, the greater your odds are of becoming an alcoholic when you're an adult.

When you're an alcoholic you develop a high tolerance to booze, so you need more and more of it to get high. You are unable to control your drinking, so once you start you can't stop. You constantly crave alcohol. And you suffer from withdrawal symptoms, like headaches, stomachaches, irritability, the shakes, sleeplessness and even delirium tremens, if you don't get a fix.

When you're an alcoholic, liquor becomes the number one priority in your life and everything and everyone else comes second. You are notoriously unreliable and untrustworthy. You don't show for important appointments, work or family obligations. And divorce and estrangement from family and friends are common. Alcohol is the love of your life.

Your life as an alcoholic consists of getting alcohol, drinking alcohol and recovering from alcohol. Nothing else matters. The life of an alcoholic is not pretty.

18. Binge Drinking Causes a Lifetime of Chronic, Deadly Health Problems

You're especially vulnerable to the toxic effects of alcohol when you're young and your body is still developing. In fact, heavy drinking when you're young could doom you to a lifetime of health problems and an early death.

Chronic liver and pancreas diseases should be your greatest concern. Booze injures your liver - making you susceptible to cirrhosis of the liver and liver cancer. You can also develop pancreatitis - a very painful condition caused and aggravated by alcohol abuse. Both of these organs are vital for life. If they're damaged beyond repair from booze, you're dead.

Spirits also cause a number of other life-threatening diseases and disorders which can affect your heart, brain, nerves and digestive tract. Simply put, bingeing when you're young can be a death sentence.

19. You Won't Look Stupid Like Your Friends Who Binge

How many times have you observed friends and acquaintances who've had one too many and act like idiots? That could be you!

Beer can make people do crazy things. Things they are ashamed and embarrassed about when they sober up. And even though your drinking pals won't admit it, they feel bad about themselves and what other people think of them after a night of hard partying.

Think about all of the stupid things your friends have said and done when they were under the influence. You don't want to come off like one of them.

20. You Won't Look Stupid Like Your Parents Who Binge

Imagine acting like your parents, if they lose control around alcohol. Slurring your words, wobbling around, bumping into things, acting irrationally. How embarrassing. You certainly don't want to follow in their footsteps.

It's time to start thinking for yourself about booze and not fall into the old drinking trap your elders have set for you. Rebelling against your parent's bad drinking example is perfectly acceptable in this case. They might even be proud of you, if you didn't binge like them.

When you look at yourself in the mirror after a night of heavy drinking, who do you see? One of your parents?

21. You Won't Pass On Alcohol Abuse to Your Kids

If you have a drinking problem and plan on becoming a parent, you might want to rethink that plan. Either clean up your act or don't reproduce because problem drinking and parenthood don't mix.

When you become a parent, your number one priority in life is your child. Everything else, including beer, comes second. You assume tons of responsibility and you simply would not be up to the job if you were a heavy drinker. Your kids would be neglected - materially and psychologically - if you were an alcohol abuser.

You're a role model for your kids too. They'd probably follow in your footsteps and learn to binge, if you binged. You'd just be bringing more little problem drinkers into the world and giving them a bad start - perhaps like your parents gave you.

You want better for your kids, don't you? Cut out binge drinking and you'll be ahead of the game.

<u>Twenty-One Great Reasons Not to Binge</u>

1. *Binge drinking prevents you from living life to the fullest*
2. *You have a natural ability to have fun without alcohol*
3. *You'll enhance your reputation if you control alcohol*
4. *You'll accent your individuality, independence and intelligence if you don't binge*
5. *You'll be happier and like yourself more if you don't binge*
6. *You're more likely to get good grades and graduate if you don't binge*
7. *You'll enjoy peace of mind not worrying about alcohol abuse*
8. *You could die from binge drinking*
9. *Binge drinking could alter the course of your life*
10. *Binge drinking could step on your good time*
11. *Binge drinking prevents you from having good friends and relationships*
12. *Binge drinking stunts your growth*
13. *Binge drinking stunts your neurological development*
14. *Binge drinking stunts your psychological development*
15. *Binge drinking stunts your social development*
16. *Binge drinking leads to sexual problems*
17. *Binge drinking leads to a life of alcoholism*
18. *Binge drinking causes a lifetime of chronic, deadly health problems*
19. *You won't look stupid like your friends who binge*
20. *You won't look stupid like your parents who binge*
21. *You won't pass on alcohol abuse to your kids*

Teaser

Imagine what your life would look like - your health, mood, family, relationships, grades, work, goals and future - if you didn't have to worry about your drinking.

From now on, every time you think about partying, think about your very good reasons to avoid bingeing. They'll motivate you to stay on the moderate drinking track.

Part III:
If You Choose To Drink, Drink Smart

Chapter Eight:
Define Your Goals and
Set Your Limits

Is drinking really right for you? Consider your abstinence and moderate drinking options. If you choose to drink, choose smart drinking - a harm reduction approach to alcohol use to avoid problems. Finally, set your goals and drink limits and you'll be set to make some positive changes.

Should You Drink?

Alcohol is so easy. It's legal, convenient, affordable, socially accepta-ble and you're happy and relaxed within minutes after a sip or two. You're pressured by others to drink too - to be cool and fit in. And you're passing from adolescence to adulthood and feeling all of the pressures and responsibilities of that transition. At times, you think liquor helps you to cope and make these changes.

You can also list lots of reasons not to drink. Booze could prevent you from having the time of your life and living up to your full potential. It could alter the course of your life, if you injured yourself or someone else or got pregnant when you're under the influence. It could eat away at your self-esteem and self-confidence and ruin your reputation. Alcohol is a toxic substance and can make you sick - hangovers, alcohol poisoning, liver and pancreas disease and brain damage. It could even kill you. Liquor causes social problems - it could alienate you from family and friends. It might cause emotional problems too - depression, anxiety and stress brought on or exacerbated by alcohol abuse. And it could cause school, work, legal and financial problems for you - lower grades, flunking out of school, getting fired from your job, getting arrested and going into debt - if you abuse it. Alcohol may be more trouble than it's worth.

If you decide not to drink for now, good for you! You've got plenty of time to make that big decision. And passing on a potentially harmful substance, like alcohol, while you're still developing physically, psychologically and socially, might be one of the best decisions you'll ever make.

If, however, you decide to drink, drink smart. Smart drinking will reduce your risk of alcohol-related problems. That's why it's called smart drinking! If you're going to drink, don't take chances. Stick to moderate drinking so you'll never have to worry about alcohol abuse or any of the heartaches that go along with it.

FYI - the legal drinking age in the United States is twenty-one. If you drink before you're twenty-one, you're breaking the law and could be arrested and jailed. You'd be wise to factor that into your "to drink or not to drink" decision.

Smart Drinking Is a Harm Reduction Approach to Alcohol Use

A harm reduction approach to alcohol use empowers you with safe drinking guidelines and skills to avoid problems. You'll learn clinically-proven behavioral, cognitive, motivational and lifestyle strategies and techniques that will enable you to drink in a sensible and moderate manner - without harming yourself or others.

Harm reduction philosophy believes that drinking is a personal choice and you are responsible for it. No one else is. And if you want to reduce or eliminate the harmful effects of liquor in your life, you can. You are capable of changing, you are capable of improving your drinking habits and you are capable of reducing your consumption, if you want to.

It's a non-judgmental approach that respects you, your intelligence and your individuality. It does not believe in the disease concept of alcoholism or that binge or problem drinking is a disease. And it is not related to Alcoholics Anonymous or the Twelve-Step program.

A harm reduction approach to alcohol use does not condone or encourage drinking. Instead, it accepts the reality that you may choose to drink - even if you're under twenty-one - and its goal is to prevent alcohol abuse, any problems associated with it and alcoholism.

What Is Smart Drinking?

Smart drinking is moderate, appropriate, problem-free drinking. It's sensible drinking suited to the occasion and it may involve food, friends and good times. Smart drinking is a drink or two with dinner, a drink or two with friends or a drink or two to celebrate a special occasion. Alcohol is never the focus and you never binge or get drunk. It's problem-free drinking and it never causes any health, psychological, social, school, work, legal or financial problems for you or anyone else.

The National Institute of Alcohol Abuse and Alcoholism (NIAAA) defines moderate drinking as no more than two drinks a day or fourteen drinks a week for men. And for women, it's no more than one drink a day or seven drinks a week. Women are allowed less alcohol because they have less of an enzyme that metabolizes alcohol, compared to men. If a woman drinks the same amount of alcohol as a man, she gets higher than a man.

Smart drinking is not bingeing, drinking as much as you can, drinking as fast as you can, drinking as often as you can, drinking to get drunk or drinking inappropriately. It's not drinking for the wrong reasons - to impress others, to cope with moods or emotions or to entertain yourself when you're lonely or bored. And you're not a smart drinker if you have any health, psychological, social, school, work, legal or financial problems caused by alcohol.

One drink is twelve ounces of beer, five ounces of wine or one and a half ounces of hard liquor. A six-pack of beer contains six drinks, a bottle of wine contains about five drinks and a half-pint of eighty proof liquor contains four drinks.

Smart Drinking Is . . .

- *Moderate drinking*
- *Appropriate drinking suited to the occasion*
- *Problem-free drinking that doesn't cause any health, psychological, social, school, work, legal or financial problems for you or anyone else*
- *Alcohol is never the focus*
- *You never binge*
- *You never get drunk*

Smart Drinking Is Not . . .

- *Bingeing*
- *Drinking to get drunk*
- *Inappropriate drinking*
- *Drinking as much as you can*
- *Drinking as fast as you can*
- *Drinking as often as you can*
- *Alcohol is the focus*
- *Drinking for the wrong reasons*
- *Drinking to impress others*
- *Drinking to cope with moods or emotions*
- *Drinking to relieve boredom and loneliness*
- *Drinking that causes any health, psychological, social, school, work, legal or financial problems for you or anyone else*

If You're Going to Drink, Set Your Daily Drink Limit

If you choose to drink smart, start by setting your daily drink limit. Why is your drink limit so important? First, when you have a drink limit in mind before you start partying, you're less likely to stray and binge. When you enter a party cold, without a limit, you often drink more than you intend. But when a limit is in place, you're less likely to overstep your bounds. Second, keeping track of your drinks will raise your drinking awareness - you'll become more aware of how much alcohol you're actually consuming. And the greater your drinking awareness, the less you'll drink - naturally.

Know your limits and you know you can have a drink or two and enjoy yourself - without getting so high your judgment becomes impaired, you're unable to say no to more liquor and you get drunk. Keep your drink limit in the back of your mind at all times and you'll feel in charge and confident. Have fun! But not too much fun.

It's decision time. Deciding what your daily drink limit will be. A daily drink limit for women should not exceed one drink. A daily drink limit for men should not exceed two drinks. And even though you have a set limit, don't feel obligated to drink your limit when you do drink or to drink every day. That kind of thinking will just keep you focused on alcohol.

Your daily drink limit is yours forever - you'll own it the rest of your life. If you always observe it, you'll never, ever, have to worry about a drinking problem again. Payoff!

Daily Drink Limits

- *Young Women - One Drink*
- *Young Men - Two Drinks*

Set Your Weekly Drink Limit Too

Now determine your weekly drink limit. Seven drinks per week for women and fourteen drinks per week for men stay within the moderate drinking guidelines set by the National Institute of Alcohol Abuse and Alcoholism. These are the weekly drink limits allowed for smart drinkers too.

Some days you shouldn't drink at all. The more abstinent days the better. Some days you're just too busy to drink and it's not appropriate. And just because you have a weekly drink limit doesn't mean you have to meet it. Stay away from booze most of the week and stick to your drink limits when you do drink and you'll have smart drinking down in no time.

Weekly Drink Limits

- *Young Women - Seven Drinks*
- *Young Men - Fourteen Drinks*

Teaser

If you choose to drink, what kind of drinker do you choose to be? A smart one? A dumb one? An out-of-control binger? Describe the type of drinker you'd like to be. Then record your daily and weekly drink limits.

Chapter Nine:
Turn On to Ten Smart Drinking Guidelines

Smart drinking is the way to go, if you're going to drink. You'll feel better, look better, have better relationships, get better grades, do better work and do better in general if you drink smart, not dumb. Follow these simple drinking guidelines and you'll be an intelligent drinker!

1. Start Thinking "Appropriate" Drinking

What's appropriate drinking? It's moderate drinking suited to the occasion and it usually involves eating and socializing. A beer with friends, a glass of wine with dinner, a glass of champagne at a wedding reception. You never drink too much, too fast or too often and you never have any problems with alcohol.

What's inappropriate drinking? It's heavy drinking that is not suited to the occasion. It's drinking because you feel pressured to, drinking to cope with feelings or drinking because you're lonely or bored. You drink too much, too fast and too often and you may develop alcohol-related problems.

From now on, any time you're tempted to start drinking, ask yourself, "Is this an appropriate drinking occasion?" If it is, observe your limits and enjoy yourself. If it isn't, avoid the situation, distract yourself, have a soft drink and don't even start.

Sensitize yourself to appropriate and inappropriate drinking. Stick to appropriate drinking and you'll master the art of smart drinking.

2. Know Your Drink Limits

If you do give yourself permission to drink in an appropriate drinking setting, always keep your daily and weekly drink limits in mind. Knowing how much you'll drink in advance increases your chances of drinking sensibly. It's that simple.

Entering a drinking party cold - without thinking about your limits - is a recipe for disaster and often leads to overdrinking. You get high, get caught up in the moment and continue drinking with no end in sight. Instead, get a grip, keep your drink limit in mind, stick to it and you can have fun - without going nuts and getting drunk.

What's your daily drink limit? One if you're a girl and two if you're a guy. What's your weekly drink limit? Seven if you're a girl and fourteen if you're a guy. Friendly reminders.

3. Limit Your Drinking Time

Knowing how long you'll drink is about as important as knowing how much you'll drink. If you have some idea of how long you'll drink before you start, the less likely you'll drink until you're drunk.

Think about it. Two drinking hours is more than enough time to enjoy yourself. Any more than that is a waste of your precious time. Less drinking time would be even better. You don't want to drink your life away!

Yes, it's possible to have a good time when you only drink an hour or two. And no, you don't have to leave a party once you've met your drink and time limits. Just switch to something lighter - non-alcoholic - and party on.

92

From now on, your drinking time limit is two hours. Every time you start to drink, look at the clock and figure out when your drinking time is up. Then stop when the time comes. After that, have a soda or mineral water. Or a hot dog or a hot fudge sundae.

Party on. Just leave out the alcohol and you'll feel great the next day.

4. Pace Your Drinking

Slowing down your drinking is also crucial for your smart drinking success. If you pace your drinking you can still live it up, but the booze won't go to your head - making it easier for you to stick to your limits and stop drinking when you should.

Slowing down sounds simple enough, but it can be a challenge when you get caught up in the moment at a party. You're talking, laughing, socializing and not thinking about pacing, so you mindlessly gulp without even thinking about it. Your cocktail is gone before you know it and you automatically have another one. You guzzle one drink after another without pacing. And you get drunk.

From now on, try to allow at least sixty minutes for each drink. The longer the better. Keep in mind it takes about an hour for most of us to metabolize the alcohol in one drink. So if you burn off the booze in one drink in one hour, you'll still have fun but you won't be getting ahead of yourself, losing control and drinking the night away.

The next time you start drinking, look at the clock. Shoot for at least sixty minutes for each drink. If that's not possible, try adding on five minutes to each drink every week until you can stay within the sixty minute time limit. In the meantime, if you finish that beer before your sixty minutes are up, don't reach for another one. Wait out the rest of your drinking time or have a soft drink instead. You'll survive and feel good about yourself if you do.

You'll love that feeling of controlling alcohol, instead of alcohol controlling you. And you won't get wasted. Do it!

5. Stick to One Drink At a Time

Keep an eye on the size of your drink too. One drink is twelve ounces of beer, five ounces of wine and one and a half ounces of hard liquor.

If you drink beer, you know you've got one drink in your hand because most beer comes in twelve ounce bottles. That's easy. If you dabble in wine, it's trickier. To get a good idea of how much one glass of wine is, pour five ounces of water in your wine glass, eyeball it and etch that amount in your brain. Then stick to that portion whenever you pour yourself a glass. Same goes for hard liquor. Pour one and a half ounces of water in a glass and make a mental note of how much it is. Next time you pour yourself a drink, stick to that amount. Or use a shot glass and measure precisely.

BTW - guzzling wine or hard liquor from the bottle or allowing your friends to make you oversized drinks are no-no's from here on out. You'll go over your limit and look like a sloppy drunk if you drink like that.

Make sure you have one and only one cocktail in your hand the next time you party. Another effortless guideline to keep you on the straight and narrow.

6. Eat Before and During Drinking

Eating is another tried and true strategy to prevent booze from going to your head. Food before and while you drink lines and protects your stomach, the alcohol isn't absorbed into your system as fast and you feel good without getting too high. You enjoy yourself, but you're still capable of stopping when you reach your limit.

Drinking on an empty stomach, on the other hand, has been the downfall of many a drinker. Alcohol rushes through your system, your blood alcohol concentration level soars, your judgment becomes impaired and you are unable to stop. You wake up the next morning with a hangover and can't remember what you said or did because you had a blackout. You drank too much on an empty stomach. Disaster!

Healthy snacks - like cheese, fruit, nuts and whole grain crackers - would be ideal. Make sure you have plenty of goodies on hand before you drink, so you don't have to scramble for them when you do.

What's on the menu the next time you drink? Whether you're drinking at home or going out, you've got to eat while you drink. No excuses!

7. Keep Most of Your Days Alcohol Free

Limiting your drinking occasions is also a terrific idea - if you want to stay in control and out of trouble with liquor.

The more you drink alcohol, the more dependent you become on it - physically and psychologically. So it only makes sense to limit your use of this potentially addictive substance. Avoid booze for a week or two or three and, if you drink during the week, limit yourself to only one or two drinking occasions. Not every day is a drinking day and if there's nothing special on your agenda, there's really no good reason to drink, is there?

If a spontaneous party does erupt, make sure you always have plenty of non-alcoholic beverages on hand and focus on alcohol-free fun, instead of drinking.

The more you limit your drinking, the smarter you'll be about it.

8. Assert Yourself Around Alcohol

What does asserting yourself around alcohol mean? It means saying what you mean and meaning what you say when it comes to booze. It's being clear to yourself and others about when, where, how much and how long you'll drink. Being assertive around liquor is a must - especially if you hang out with people who pressure you to drink.

If you choose to drink, but want to pace yourself and stop after a couple, say so. If you choose not to drink at all, say so. If you don't want beer forced on you, say so. That's being assertive about booze.

You don't have to be rude when you speak your mind. Be polite, but firm. "No thanks", "I'm fine" or "I've had my limit" are smart drinking phrases you can use on people who want you to party on.

You can be assertive non-verbally too. Cover your drink with your hand or napkin. Push away your drink or set it down and walk away. Sooner or later, others will get the message.

And if hard drinking pals continue to pester you to drink, give them a good excuse. An honest one would be best. You're working out tomorrow. Or you've got a big exam in the morning. Or you're driving. Or you want to lose weight. Or you're wrapping up a big project at work. Or you've got a no-drinking contract with your parents.

If an honest excuse doesn't get them off your back, you should question your choice of friends. Do you want to associate with people who can't take no for an answer? Is drinking the only common interest you share with these pals? Is it time to move on?

Practice your smart drinking phrases, non-verbal communication and excuses before a big drinking bash. Practice makes perfect. And you'll feel more comfortable refusing drinks when the time comes.

Speak up and control alcohol! At the end of the day, you and only you are responsible for starting drinking and stopping drinking.

9. Put Alcohol in Perspective

Think of the most important things in your life. Fun, freedom, your girlfriend or boyfriend, your family, friends, school, money, achieving your goals, working, your future. Does alcohol make your top ten? Top twenty? If it does, you're spending too much valuable time drinking or thinking about drinking.

Beer is just a complement to your fabulous life. It shouldn't BE your life. If you're placing too much importance on liquor and its effects, you need an attitude adjustment. An alcohol attitude adjustment where you put booze in its place - at the bottom of your "most important things in my life" list. You'll effortlessly drink less if you do.

How does alcohol fit into the big picture of your life? What are the top twenty "most important" feelings, people, places, things and goals in your life? If liquor is on the list, every time you think of drinking, fight back. Mentally put it down on the bottom of your list, then go out and have some good, clean alcohol-free fun.

10. Know When the Alcohol Is Talking

So, you've had a cocktail and you're thinking about having another one. You feel relaxed, happy and you're ready for some action.

You think you're fine - capable of making wise decisions, including wise decisions about drinking. You may even think you can drive. But you're wrong. You're physically and psychologically impaired and you're experiencing an alcohol-altered reality. A reality that tells you you're capable of almost anything - when you're not. At this point, you're under the influence, caught up in the moment, the liquor is talking to you and you're no longer in charge, alcohol is.

Separate your alcohol-impaired mindset from reality. The truth is your perception and thought processes are off when you're high and you're not capable of making great decisions about anything, including drinking or driving. Acknowledge booze is playing with your mind. Maybe that will bring you back to the real world.

Do you know when alcohol is talking to you? The next time you drink, listen to it, then dismiss it - especially when it's telling you to have more beer.

Ten Smart Drinking Guidelines

1. *Start thinking "appropriate" drinking*
2. *Know your drink limits*
3. *Limit your drinking time*
4. *Pace your drinking*
5. *Stick to one drink at a time*
6. *Eat before and during drinking*
7. *Keep most of your days alcohol free*
8. *Assert yourself around alcohol*
9. *Put alcohol in perspective*
10. *Know when the alcohol is talking*

Teaser

Memorize and observe your smart drinking guidelines this week. Which ones come easy? Which ones will you have to work on? What are you telling yourself to put alcohol in perspective? What are you telling yourself when the alcohol is talking?

Chapter Ten:
Turn On to Twenty-Five Smart Drinking Tips Too

Here are some simple tips to drink smart, not dumb. Try each one at least two times, then decide which ones work best for you and keep practicing them. If you do, you'll develop a large repertoire of behavior management skills to moderate alcohol and you'll enjoy smart drinking forever!

1. Devise a Smart Drinking Plan for Every Drinking Occasion

So far, you've made some important decisions about your drinking. You've set your drink limits, you've set your drinking time limit, you'll pace each drink, you'll measure each drink, you'll eat before and during drinking and you'll be assertive around alcohol. Now you'll learn how to make a smart drinking plan that takes all of these variables into account. If you have a smart drinking plan in place before you start sipping, you're more likely to stay within your drink limits and avoid problem drinking.

Say there's a big bash on Friday night. You know beer will be flowing. And you know everyone there will be drinking - some people will be bingeing and getting drunk. But you don't want to be one of those drinkers, so you develop a smart drinking plan for the party to be on the safe side.

First, you'll decide how many drinks you'll have. That's easy. Your limit - one or two drinks. Second, you'll figure out how long you'll drink alcohol at this bash. Two hours - tops. Third, you'll keep an eye on your drink portions - making sure you only have one drink at a time. Fourth, you'll watch the clock and allow at least sixty minutes for each drink. Longer, if possible. Fifth, you'll eat a hearty meal before you arrive and take snacks in case there's no food. Sixth, when you've reached your drink limit and your drinking time is up, you'll practice your assertive drinking skills and refuse more liquor. Seventh, you'll either leave the party or switch to non-alcoholic drinks and activities and keep playing. Your smart drinking plan in a nutshell.

Get the idea? Making a drinking plan before you make the rounds may be the secret to your smart drinking success. From now on, devise a drinking plan before every drinking occasion - and smart drinking will come naturally.

Devise Your Seven Step Smart Drinking Plan

1. *Know your drink limit*
2. *Know your drinking time limit*
3. *Stick to one drink portions*
4. *Allow sixty minutes for each drink*
5. *Eat before and during drinking*
6. *Be assertive and refuse more alcohol*
7. *Leave the party or stay and switch to non-alcoholic drinks and activities*

2. Stick to Your Smart Drinking Plan

All the drinking plans in the world are meaningless unless you stick to them and make them work for you. They're just words that you give meaning to when you follow through with them. Words and plans are powerful, but actions are more powerful.

Be proactive, put your plan into action when the time comes and reap the benefits of smart drinking - feeling good and feeling good about yourself in the morning.

3. Perfect the Polite Refusal

If your friends hound you to drink and get drunk, even though you don't want to, it's time you learned the art of the polite refusal - nicely, but firmly, saying no to a cocktail. Learning to say no to booze is a must if you're going to resist peer pressure to drink.

"No thanks." "I'm good right now." "I'm taking a time out." "I don't drink." "Please stop pressuring me. I've already said no." "Can I have some soda instead?" Choose phrases you feel comfortable with or make up some of your own and practice them, silently or out loud, when no one's looking. When you've got your polite refusals down, saying no to more alcohol will be effortless. And your friend or server will get the message and stop forcing beer on you.

But if they persist in getting you liquored up even after you've said no, try giving them a good reason why you don't want to drink. An honest excuse would be best. Tell them you're tired and ready to turn in for the night. Tell them you've got a big test, game or project the next day and can't have a hangover. Tell them you've made a contract with your parents not to drink and drive. Tell them you're high enough and more would put you under the table. Tell them whatever you feel like telling them to get them off your back. Have a good excuse on hand and maybe your pals will stop bugging you. If they don't, leave.

What do your polite refusals and excuses sound like? Practice them right now. Then insert them into your smart drinking plan when needed so you can stay within your drink limit. Eventually, saying no to alcohol will get easier and easier.

Polite Refusals and Excuses

- *"No thanks."*
- *"I'm fine right now."*
- *"I'm taking a time out."*
- *"I've had my limit."*
- *"I'm not drinking tonight."*
- *"I don't drink."*
- *"Please stop pestering me to drink."*
- *"Can I have a soda instead?"*
- *"I'm tired and going home."*
- *"I have a big test tomorrow."*
- *"I have a big game tomorrow."*
- *"I don't want a hangover tomorrow."*
- *"I don't drink and drive."*
- *"I'm high enough."*

4. Resist the Social Pressure to Drink

Everybody's drinking and they seem to be enjoying themselves. Some people are even getting smashed. And they want you to join in and drink as much and as recklessly as they're drinking. You feel pressured. You want to fit in. You want to be liked. You want to be popular. And sometimes you think heavy drinking is the price you must pay to have friends and have fun.

If you base your social success on how much and how often you drink, you've got a problem. Three problems really. A drinking problem. You're probably drinking too much for no good reason. A social problem. You're keeping company with the wrong crowd - people who value you for your alcohol consumption. And a self-esteem problem. You don't think you're good enough to be liked without booze.

How can you resist the pressure to drink? First, by becoming aware of it. The more aware you are of it, the less susceptible you'll be to it. Second, by pumping up your self-esteem and telling yourself you don't need beer to fit in or to be liked. You're better than that.

Three, stop hanging out with the wrong crowd that respects booze more than they respect you. Make friends with people who like you for you, not for how many shots you can down. And four, make a smart drinking plan in advance for all social drinking occasions. Be sure to include plenty of polite refusals and excuses about why you don't want to get wasted. Then follow through with your plan.

How much social pressure do you face around alcohol? On a scale from one to ten, with one being the least amount of peer pressure and ten being the most, how do you rate? If you're under five, it should be simple to shrug off that pressure and not over drink at parties. If it's five or more, it's more difficult to resist the pull of the crowd and it's something for you to work on.

If you can take the pressure out of the peer pressure to drink - a huge influence on most young people - you can become a smart drinker. Sweet!

Resist Peer Pressure to Drink

- *Be aware of it*
- *Pump up your self-esteem*
- *Don't hang with people who pressure you to drink*
- *Devise a smart drinking plan*
- *Practice your polite refusals and/or excuses*
- *Follow through with your smart drinking plan*

5. **Polish Up Your Drinking Style**

Maybe you gulp that drink, instead of sipping it. Maybe you don't pace yourself and down that beer in ten or fifteen minutes. Maybe you always have a drink in your hand, never putting it down and giving yourself a break. Nasty little drinking habits that add up to too much liquor, too fast.

Clean up those nasty little habits while you still can. In the future, sip, don't gulp. Swill too much booze at a time and it goes to your head. Sipping your cocktail is an effortless way to slow down and not lose it.

Pace yourself and wait at least five minutes between sips too. You'll still enjoy the effects of the alcohol, but you won't get loaded.

And get that drink out of your hand. Yes, put it down between sips. You'll be less likely to drink it so fast and more likely to stick to your drink limit.

Polishing up your drinking style is not rocket science and shows you're in charge. Add your spiffy new drinking habits to your drinking plan when the time comes and smart drinking will come naturally.

Polish Up Your Drinking Style

- *Sip, don't gulp*
- *Pace yourself and wait five minutes between sips*
- *Put your drink down between sips*

6. Delay First and Successive Drinks

Good things come to those who wait. Wait to drink that is. You don't consume as much liquor, you stay in control, you're more likely to stick to your drink limit and you feel good about yourself for exercising a little restraint. Payoffs!

Try waiting on that first drink. It won't kill you to delay it by ten, twenty or thirty minutes. In fact, you might even be proud of yourself. You've got enough self-control to resist alcohol!

Delay between drinks too. Instead of mindlessly having one drink after another, plan on a ten, twenty or thirty minute break between beers. An hour break would be great. You like yourself so much more when you control alcohol.

Add delaying first and successive drinks to your smart drinking plan when needed. It works!

7. Start with a Non-Alcoholic Drink

Why do you have to have a beer right out of the gate? You don't! Have a non-alcoholic beverage for starters instead. Enjoy a soda, juice, water, latte or tea when you're tempted to start drinking. An alcohol-free beverage will distract you from drinking, you'll strengthen your self-control muscles and you'll stick to your drink limit. More payoffs!

The trick is to make sure you've got plenty of your favorite non-alcoholic drinks on hand. That way you won't have any excuses to start with tequila. And take soft drinks with you when you go out too. Stuff them in your bag or backpack. Then you won't have to scramble for one, if they're not available at the party.

Incorporate this handy non-alcoholic starter tip into your smart drinking plan. It's a no-brainer.

8. Alternate with Non-Alcoholic Drinks

Enjoy non-alcoholic drinks between alcoholic ones too. Sparkling water, soda or juice? You'll still have fun - you're a little high and metabolizing the booze you already have in your system. But you won't be getting ahead of yourself - as far as the liquor is concerned.

Add this tip to your smart drinking repertoire and see how easy staying within your drink limits can be. Hello smart drinking, goodbye hangovers!

9. Switch Drinks

If you drink hard liquor, switch to something a little lighter, like beer or wine. Only one and a half ounces of distilled alcohol is considered one drink. That's not a lot. That small amount goes a long way, but it's gone in no time. You get too high, too fast and your smart drinking plan goes out the window.

Five ounces of wine and twelve ounces of beer, on the other hand, are larger portions. You can sip on wine or beer for a while because you've got more of it. And you won't get so high so fast - so you're still able to stick to your plan and not get drunk.

If you insist on the hard stuff, dilute it with lots of mixer and ice. The more watered down it is, the better and hopefully, you won't go bananas.

Downsize from distilled liquor to beer or wine and you'll down-size your risk of problem drinking. Play with this tip and put it in your smart drinking plan when needed.

10. Keep Busy At Drinking Parties

When you're out, don't focus on the beer. That's not smart drinking. Staring at that beer and concentrating on finishing it will just make you drunk.

Turn your attention to the people and activities happening around you instead. Get into the conversation and energy and you'll distract yourself from drinking. As a result, you'll drink slower and won't get pounded.

Next time you hit the social scene, focus on the conversation, people, games, singing, dancing and joke-telling. Enjoy the process, not the booze. You'll be amazed at how simple it will be to stick to your limit.

Add this tip to your smart drinking plan - especially if social drinking gets you in trouble.

11. Don't Do Shots

You're crazy if you think you can do straight shots of hard liquor and still be a smart drinker. Just a couple of shots of tequila, vodka, schnapps, rum, scotch, bourbon or whiskey and you're high as a kite and out of control.

In addition to getting smashed, you'll probably have a blackout too - you won't have any memory the next day of what you said or did during the rest of the drinking party. And of course, you'll have a hangover.

Be kind to yourself and others and don't do shots. It's just not worth the hangover, blackout, brain damage, embarrassment, shame and stigma you'll feel the next day.

12. Don't Play Drinking Games

Another no-brainer. The number one way to lose control and get tanked is to make a game out of drinking. But drinking contests and competitions are not all fun and games. They're serious business because too much booze can be deadly - causing alcohol poisoning, accidents, suicide and homicide.

All drinking games are off limits from now on. No exceptions.

13. Don't Drink to Get Drunk

Drinkers who binge often have an "all or nothing at all" attitude about alcohol. They think you either don't drink at all or you drink to get drunk. There is no in-between or happy medium for them. This black and white thinking about liquor is a problem because every time they drink, they think they have to get smashed.

If you suffer from this mindset, do something about it. Tell yourself you're capable of having good times on one or two drinks and you don't have to binge and get drunk just because you have one beer. Moderate drinking. What a concept.

Talk yourself out of this black and white thinking about alcohol and you'll talk yourself into smart drinking.

14. Adopt An "I Don't Need Alcohol" Attitude

How do you cultivate an "I don't need alcohol" attitude? First, you tell yourself you don't need booze to feel good about yourself, to be sociable, to fit in, to be popular, to have fun or to cope with feelings. Then you tell yourself you've got the intelligence and good judgment to successfully handle anything that comes your way - without alcohol. Think this. Feel this. Own this. And give yourself this pep talk every day - especially when you're facing a drinking party.

Believe in yourself. You can survive and thrive - without liquor. Every smart drinker knows this. And when you adopt an "I don't need alcohol" attitude, you'll know it too.

15. Get Busy On the Weekends

Ah, the weekends. No school, no work, free time, party time. Do you reserve your weekends for drinking? Do you zone out all weekend, then get back to business on Monday morning?

If weekend partying is killing you, start doing things differently. Line up lots of alcohol-free activities for Saturday and Sunday. Play, exercise, relax, challenge yourself - but don't include beer. Pack your weekends with interesting things to do, not six-packs.

Go to the beach, learn tai chi, cook, join a softball team, go to a concert, play chess, get a massage, explore caves, have people over for dinner, stay in bed, go to an art exhibit. Think about what would pleasure you and do it.

And stop thinking it's okay to binge on the weekends. It isn't. Enjoying lots of alcohol-free activities is an important aspect of a smart drinking lifestyle. Add it to your smart drinking plans.

16. Make Sane New Drinking Friends

It's a lot easier to stick to drink limits and not binge if you hang out with people who stick to drink limits and don't binge. These sane drinkers aren't obsessed with alcohol and booze is never the highlight of a social occasion for them. Drinking is not required for a good time or to earn their friendship. These people are intelligent, independent and reliable. They're good friend material.

How can you cultivate friendships with worthwhile people who don't have drinking problems? Connect with people who have the same alcohol-free interests you have and get acquainted with friends of sane drinking friends. Just two ways to meet people of like mind and drinking habits.

Strike up relationships with smart drinking people and moderate drinking will be a cinch.

17. Appoint a Designated Driver

If you choose to drink at a party, make sure you have a designated driver on hand before you even take a sip of alcohol. Drinking - even if it's just one drink - and driving don't mix. Don't even think about drinking unless you know you have a safe way of getting home with a non-drinker.

And if your designated driver starts drinking or flakes out on you, take public transportation or call a cab. It's a lot less hassle than being arrested for drunk driving and it's a lot less expensive than court fines, lawyer's fees, drunk driving school and increased insurance premiums incurred from a DUI or DWI.

BTW, having a designated driver doesn't mean you can drink in excess or get tanked. That's not smart thinking or drinking.

18. Consider Your Feelings Before Drinking

Don't expose yourself to a drinking party when you're hungry or tired. Don't challenge yourself with a drinking party when you're in a bad mood. When you're not quite one-hundred percent - physically or psychologically - you're more susceptible to binge or problem drinking. You drink more beer to feel better.

Attend drinking events only when you're up to it - when you feel good physically and mentally. The better you feel, the less you'll drink.

19. Rethink Heavy Drinking Occasions

You don't have to attend every keg party you're invited to. If you know it's going to be a free-for-all, it certainly increases your chances of getting loaded. You do have the option of not going and doing something else. And you don't have to socialize until the break of dawn. The later you stay out, the longer you might drink and the more likely you'll get drunk.

Feel free to leave a drinking party when the mood strikes you too. You don't have to stay until the bitter end. Leave - if the party gets out of hand or you start to feel uncomfortable. You'll be less likely to get wasted.

From now on, before you even hit a drinking event, you'll consciously decide to go or not to go, how long you'll stay and when you'll leave. You'll reduce your binge or problem drinking risk if you do.

20. Remind Yourself the Effects of Alcohol Reinforce Continued Drinking

Yes, you feel great after a drink or two. You calm down and everything looks rosy. But the better you feel, the more you want to drink. It's a never ending cycle. You drink, you feel good, you want more booze to continue to feel good, you drink, you feel good, and you continue to drink and so on. And the cycle doesn't stop until you're seeing pink elephants or you put your foot down and quit.

Become aware of this cycle and outsmart it. Recognize what's happening to you and put an end to it when you reach your drink limit. Who's in control? You or alcohol? You are and don't forget it!

21. Don't Always Equate Alcohol with a Good Time

If you think beer always makes for a good time, think again. Sure, sometimes when you're mildly high you have fun and enjoy yourself. But there are lots of bad things that happen when you and your pals drink too. Arguments, fist fights, dangerous situations. Liquor can often lead to some pretty awful predicaments.

You probably have a selective memory when it comes to alcohol and good times. Just remind yourself that booze and being under the influence don't always add up to fun or make you happy. Understand this and you'll drink less automatically.

22. Don't Control Your Inside Feelings with Outside Substances

Do you know what you're doing when you're drinking? Especially when you're bingeing? You're trying to regulate your inner feelings with an outside substance - alcohol in this case. And trying to feel better from the outside in just doesn't work. It wears off when the liquor wears off. Fixing yourself from the inside out is much more effective and lasts longer too.

Once you've got this down, every time you pick up a beer you'll have second thoughts about it. A smart drinking thing to do!

23. Deciding When to Stop Drinking - Made Easy

When you're drinking, take a step back before every cocktail and think about how high you are. Then think about how many drinks you've had, what your limit is and ask yourself two questions. Am I high enough? If you say no to this question, then ask yourself if you've reached your limit. If you answer yes to either one of these questions, you're done drinking. It's that simple.

Take a step back when you drink and you'll be taking a step towards smart drinking.

24. Make the Most of a Mistake

So you blew it and went over your drink limit the last time you partied. And now you're paying for it with guilt and a hangover.

This is no time to throw in the towel. Not yet, at least. This is the time to get with the program - the Beat Binge Drinking Program - more than ever. Leave the guilt and shame of your drinking mistake behind and get back on track immediately. And learn from your mistake - review the circumstances that triggered it, make plans to avoid the same mistake in the future and get on with your sensible drinking life.

When you change a habit or behavior, it's normal to slip up every once in a while. But the idea is to learn from your slips so they never happen again and keep working the program until you've achieved your problem-free, moderate drinking goal.

Don't be defeated by a drinking mistake. Changing drinking behavior is a process and a slip is part of that process. Learn your lesson and carry on.

25. Simplify Your Life and Stop Drinking

If you slip often or you slip for long periods of time you'd be wise to consider not drinking at all. If you have a hard time sticking to your drink limits, you go overboard frequently or you have any health, psychological, social, school, work, legal or financial problems associated with your drinking, moderate drinking isn't working for you. Be honest with yourself and get on with your life without booze.

Eliminating your struggle with alcohol would simplify your life. You wouldn't have to worry about drink limits, drinking time, what drives you to drink, etc. Abstinence would be easier - and healthier - for you than trying to control your drinking. Think about it.

Twenty-Five Smart Drinking Tips

1. *Devise a smart drinking plan for every drinking occasion*
2. *Stick to your smart drinking plan*
3. *Perfect the polite refusal*
4. *Resist the social pressure to drink*
5. *Polish up your drinking style*
6. *Delay first and successive drinks*
7. *Start with a non-alcoholic drink*
8. *Alternate with non-alcoholic drinks*
9. *Switch drinks*
10. *Keep busy at drinking parties*
11. *Don't do shots*
12. *Don't play drinking games*
13. *Don't drink to get drunk*
14. *Adopt an "I don't need alcohol" attitude*
15. *Get busy on the weekends*
16. *Make sane new drinking friends*
17. *Appoint a designated driver*
18. *Consider your feelings before partying*
19. *Rethink heavy drinking occasions*
20. *Remind yourself the effects of alcohol reinforce continued drinking*

21. *Don't always equate alcohol with a good time*
22. *Don't control your inside feelings with outside substances*
23. *Deciding when to stop drinking - made easy*
24. *Make the most of a mistake*
25. *Simplify your life and stop drinking*

Teaser

What tips will you incorporate into your smart drinking plans? Into your drinking behavior and lifestyle? Write them down. Practice them. Own them. And you'll have no problems with alcohol.

Part IV:
Now Dig A Little Deeper
To Prevent Binge Drinking

Chapter Eleven:
What Triggers Your Drinking? Fix It!

Did you know that certain things - people, places, circumstances and feelings - can trigger your drinking? But you can control these things - drinking cues - so they don't lead to binge or problem drinking?

Here you'll learn to identify your drinking cues. Then you'll learn five ways you can defuse them so they don't trigger problem drinking. And finally, you'll learn about your perfect storm of drinking cues and your binge drinking cycle - and how to deal with them so you can stay can within your drink limits.

Control your drinking cues and you'll control your drinking!

First, Get to Know Your External Drinking Cues

External drinking cues are people, places, things, sights and smells that switch on your desire to drink. The more you're aware of them, the less vulnerable you'll be to them.

Drinking Companions

Yes, the people you hang with can have a huge effect on you - including how much and how often you drink. If your friends think they have to get smashed to make a party a party, that's a problem. If they think they have to get wasted every weekend and want to include you, that's a problem. And if you have to drink whenever you socialize with them, that's a problem. These friends encourage you to drink heavily and they're drinking cues for you.

How do you handle people who start you drinking and keep you drinking? First, you evaluate your relationship with them. Then you either phase them out of your life, limit the time you spend with them or change the way you think about them, so they don't continue to support your problem drinking.

What's your relationship like with problem drinking pals? What do you have in common with them, other than alcohol? If beer is the only thing that bonds you, stop seeing them. They're more trouble than they're worth.

If there's more to the relationship than just liquor, limit the time you spend with them. You can still enjoy their company, but you won't fall into the old drinking trap they set for you. How about socializing with them for only two or three hours, instead of five or six? Limit your time with them and limit your drinking.

Suggest no drinking or smart drinking to them too. Who knows? They might just go for it and everyone could eliminate their "drinking problem". You'll all drink smart. No worries.

If breaking ties or limiting your time with drinking pals doesn't work, try changing the way you think about them. Do you really want to associate with people whose only goal in life is to get loaded? You don't. They're losers. You want to run with a better, more interesting crowd. With this mindset you'll be bored with these jerks in no time and move on to a smarter, more ambitious crowd who keeps booze to a minimum. Change your mind, change your friends, change your drinking habits.

What friends of yours always have a drink in their hand? What people do you hang out with who think drinking and getting drunk are normal pastimes? Then think about how you'll handle them so they don't encourage your problem drinking.

Drinking Places

Do you do most of your drinking at home? At friend's homes? At your fraternity or sorority house? At a favorite club or restaurant? Down by the creek or behind the barn? At the local pizza parlor or pub? Or downtown, where nobody knows you? If you drink and get drunk at certain places, those places are drinking cues for you.

How do you handle spots that start you drinking and keep you drinking? You avoid or limit your time in these places. They push your drinking buttons - you associate booze, drinking and maybe even getting drunk with these places. And even though they're just ordinary venues for most people, they pose a threat to you.

If avoiding them or limiting your time at them doesn't work, change the way you think about locations that put you at risk. Is your home a bar and a place to get drunk? No. It's a place to rest, relax and recharge, not make yourself sick on beer. Is it appropriate for you to get smashed at your pal's apartment? No. Your pal's apartment is a place to socialize, study and cook together, not get wasted. If you get intoxicated at your fraternity or sorority house, you shouldn't. It's your home, study area and social club, not a place to abuse alcohol. And when you go out to eat or go clubbing, should liquor be your focus? It shouldn't be. You should be focusing on other activities - eating, talking, socializing, dancing and having a good time - and putting tequila on the back burner. Change the way you think about a harmful drinking cue and you'll drink less.

Where do you give yourself permission to drink? Where do you give yourself permission to get drunk? Dangerous places. And it's up to you to deal with them so they don't trigger binge or problem drinking.

Drinking Circumstances

Parties, dates, sporting events, fraternity or sorority functions, business meetings, weekends, hanging out with friends, celebrations, spring break, weddings, homecoming? Are these occasions just excuses for you to drink and get tanked? If they are, they're drinking cues for you.

When you're at one of these special events you get carried away. Liquor is flowing and everyone's guzzling. You lose it and smart drinking becomes the furthest thing from your mind.

For the time being, try avoiding these situations altogether until you feel you have moderate drinking under your belt. If you don't attend these risky functions for a month or two, you'll eliminate the temptation of drinking in excess, you'll be interrupting your old problem drinking pattern and it will be easier for you to control yourself when you do get back into the swing of things. Take some time off from these heavy drinking events and you'll be taking some time off from problem drinking too.

But if avoiding these occasions is impossible, limit the time you spend at them. If you're going to a party where beer will be the main attraction, plan in advance to stay only two or three hours tops. You don't have to drink the night away, like you use to. Or if you're watching a game or just passing time with friends, again, limit your time. Drinking endlessly at any social event just invites alcohol abuse.

If eliminating or limiting your exposure to high-risk drinking circumstances isn't helping you to manage alcohol any better, change the way you think about the social function. Is the point of a party to get drunk? No. It's to socialize, dance and enjoy yourself. It's not the wine. Is the point of watching a game to get wasted? No. It's to watch the game. It's not the beer. Is the point of laying around on Friday night to get loaded? No. It's to relax. It's not the vodka. Do you have to get smashed every weekend? No. It's your time to have some good, clean fun, like hiking, going to a concert or baking chocolate chip cookies. It's not the booze. Focus on the real purpose of the event, not the alcohol, and remember - a drinking occasion is never an excuse to get drunk.

What social functions trigger your drinking? Which ones have you gotten drunk at? Learn from your mistakes and the next time you attend a risky drinking party make sure you have your smart drinking plan on hand.

Drinking Sights, Sounds and Smells

Just seeing alcohol, smelling alcohol or hearing alcohol being poured may trigger your drinking. People toasting margaritas next to you at a restaurant. The smell of liquor at a bar. Seeing beer every time you open the refrigerator door. Passing by the wine rack in the kitchen. Careful, these may be drinking cues for you.

Just knowing these cues could spark your drinking desire will put them in perspective for you and reduce your craving. Remember, they're really only sights, sounds and smells. Nothing more. Next, eliminate or limit your exposure to these drinking cues and change the way you think about them too. Hide the beer in the refrigerator, so you don't see it every time you open the door. Bring out the bottle of wine, only when you plan on opening it. And savor the enchiladas at the Mexican restaurant, not the tequila.

The next time you're seduced by booze, get a hold of yourself. You're only thinking about drinking because you see the beer, you smell the tequila or you hear the mixed drink being poured. You'll get over it!

Do the sights, sounds and smells of alcohol stimulate your need to drink? Become aware of how they affect you and you'll cut down automatically.

External Drinking Cues

- *Drinking companions*
- *Drinking places*
- *Drinking circumstances*
- *Drinking sights, sounds and smells*

Get to Know Your Internal Drinking Cues Too

Internal drinking cues are a little harder to spot than external ones. They're sensations, feelings and moods - sometimes not obvious. But you can sensitize yourself to them and manage them - by treating them appropriately and weakening or eliminating them or changing the way you think about them - so they don't get you in trouble with alcohol.

Physiological Sensations

When you're hungry, tired, thirsty or in pain, your defenses are down and you may turn to booze for a quick fix - to fill up, perk up, quench your thirst or ease your pain. These physiological sensations could be drinking cues for you and you may not even know it.

How do you handle these cues so they don't lead to overdrinking? First, you tune into them and recognize they might trigger a drinking response in you. Being aware that a physiological sensation may a drinking cue for you is a good start.

Then you treat the cue appropriately. Eat, if you're hungry. Chill out or nap, if you're tired. Drink water if you're thirsty and take an aspirin or see your doctor if you're hurting. Satisfying physical needs appropriately will weaken or eliminate the cue and your need to drink.

Change your mind about the cue too. Tell yourself these sensations have nothing to do with alcohol and drinking is not a healthy response to them. Talk back to meeting your physical needs with booze and problem drinking will no longer be a knee jerk reaction.

Do physiological sensations start you drinking? Which ones lead to binge or problem drinking for you? How will you handle them in the future so they're no longer a threat to your smart drinking habits?

Feelings and Moods

Do you drink when you're happy or sad or both? Do you drink when you're stressed, depressed, anxious, angry or frustrated? Do you drink when you're lonely or bored? Do you drink to cope with a miserable home life or bad relationship? Do you drink to rebel? Do you drink to celebrate? Whether you're up or you're down, do you turn to alcohol to improve your mood? Obviously, emotions and states of mind are powerful drinking cues for many drinkers, including young drinkers.

When you feel good, you use liquor to feel a little bit better. And maybe one or two drinks will enhance your good mood. But three or four won't and you'll pay for it the next day.

When you're down, you use booze to lift your spirits or numb out. And one or two drinks might do the trick. But too much will make you feel even worse. Alcohol is not an appropriate or permanent solution for negative feelings and nursing emotions with liquor doesn't work long-term. It only leads to alcoholism.

And if you're struggling with a serious psychological problem, like stress, depression or anxiety, instead of hitting the bottle, you need to put together a plan or get professional help to feel better. First, you have to sit down and recognize your feelings. Then you have to identify the reasons causing these feelings. Next, you have to research and brainstorm solutions to the problems behind your feelings. And finally, you have to follow through with the best solutions - so you no longer turn to alcohol to cope or medicate.

Handling feelings and moods on your own might be difficult or impossible at times. Sometimes you're too close to the forest to see the trees. That's when you should bring someone else into the picture - a school counselor, psychologist, physician, clergyman or trusted friend. Maybe they can help you tackle and overcome the dark moods that drive you to drink.

What emotions, moods or states of mind trigger your drinking? How will you deal with them, so they don't trip problem drinking? A smart drinker never lets feelings dictate his or her drinking behavior.

Internal Drinking Cues

- *Physiological sensations*
- *Emotions*
- *Moods and states of mind*

More On Five Methods to Manage Your Drinking Cues . . .

Psychologists say you can defuse internal and external cues five different ways so they don't lead to undesirable behavior, like binge or problem drinking. Master these methods and you'll master smart drinking.

1. Handle the Cue Appropriately

Eat if you're hungry, instead of drinking. Sleep if you're tired, instead of drinking. Drink water if you're thirsty, instead of drinking. And take an aspirin or call the doc if you're in pain, instead of drinking. All perfect examples of satisfying potentially dangerous drinking cues appropriately - without reaching for a beer.

2. Eliminate the Cue

Another way to manage a drinking cue is to simply eliminate it. For example, if your friends want you to party all weekend long and get drunk, stop hanging out with them. It may be hard in the beginning because they're your buddies. But you know it would be healthier for you in the long run to stop seeing them.

True, it might be difficult to avoid or eliminate people, places and circumstances that trigger your drinking at first. Expect to feel a little uncomfortable when you make a break. That's normal. But it will get easier and easier over time. And you'll feel better - physically and psychologically - if you get rid of drinking cues that encourage bad habits.

3. Limit Your Exposure to the Cue

You can also limit the time you're exposed to the drinking cue, so it doesn't lead to binge or problem drinking. If you decide cutting ties with your weekend partying pals is out of the question, do things differently. Socialize with them on only one day - like Friday or Saturday - but not the entire weekend. And cut down on the time you spend with them when you do get together. Instead of having an open-ended party, cut down to two or three hours then leave. You can still have a relationship with your hard drinking friends, but you won't be drinking for days like you use to.

When you limit your exposure to a drinking cue you can still have a good time, but you'll reduce your risk of heavy drinking.

4. Weaken the Cue

When you weaken a drinking cue, you weaken its effect on you and your alcohol appetite. Satisfying physiological cues appropriately will weaken them. Like eating or sleeping, if you're hungry or tired. And feelings and moods that drive you to drink can be weakened by resolving the issues behind them.

Some drinking cues will never be eliminated or fixed and the best you can hope for is to lessen their effect. A weak drinking cue is better than a strong one! It's manageable. And it makes your drinking more manageable too.

5. Change the Way You Perceive and Think About the Cue

Another way to handle a drinking cue so it doesn't lead to dumb drinking is to change the way you look at it. For example, if cutting ties or limiting your time with your weekend partying buds isn't working, change the way you perceive and think about them and the situation. You may not have a lot in common with these people besides beer. You may not share any interests or have any reason to get together with them except to drink. These people are losers. And getting wasted every weekend is no longer your idea of fun. Now you're into more stimulating experiences than just sitting around and getting drunk. It's time for you to move on. Moving away from problem drinking people and activities and moving towards healthy people and activities.

Change the ways you perceive and think about dangerous drinking cues and you'll change the way perceive and think about drinking and alcohol.

Five Ways to Defuse Drinking Cues

1. *Handle the cue appropriately*
2. *Eliminate the cue*
3. *Limit your exposure to the cue*
4. *Weaken the cue*
5. *Change the way you perceive and think about the cue*

What's Your Perfect Storm of Drinking Cues?

Did you know that every drinker, including you, may fall victim to a unique set of internal and external drinking cues that triggers their drinking? And when they encounter this perfect storm of people, places, circumstances, physiological and psychological factors, they give themselves permission to binge and get drunk?

Say you've had a bad day, you're at a party with heavy drinking pals who pressure you to drink, plus you're hungry and tired. You could probably successfully deal with each of one of these cues individually and not binge. But when they're all combined, you're overwhelmed, you let yourself go and permit yourself to paint the town.

What's your perfect storm of drinking cues? When was the last time you drank too much or binged? What was the cue combination that led to your downfall? Be specific about the people, places and circumstances and your physiological and psychological states.

The next time you encounter your perfect storm of drinking cues, step back, realize you're in the midst of your perfect storm, then deal with each cue individually so they don't get to you and your alcohol consumption. You'll not only quiet your perfect storm, you'll prevent problem drinking too.

Devise a smart drinking plan for your perfect storm right now and you'll have no excuse for drinking too much when it rages.

Defeat Your Binge or Problem Drinking Cycle At Any Stage

If you knew what your binge or problem drinking cycle looked like, you might just be able to defeat it and avoid going to that dark alcohol abuse place. The smarter you are about your drinking cycle, the smarter you'll be about drinking.

The first stage of your drinking cycle always starts with a special set of circumstances - your perfect storm of internal and external drinking cues. Maybe it's Friday night and friends are drinking and encouraging you to join in. You've had a long day and you're hungry and tired. Maybe you're stressed over school or work too. All of these drinking cues combine to become your perfect storm which will start you drinking - unless you take steps to defuse them. You can stop the cycle at this stage by going home, going to bed, eating or realizing you're vulnerable to problem drinking because you're stressed out.

The second stage of your drinking cycle is the drinking thinking stage - you're making up excuses to drink and get drunk. Here's another opportunity to avert a drinking disaster. Simply talk back to your drinking thinking and remind yourself of all of your very good reasons not to binge and to stick to moderate drinking instead. You could prevent an alcohol meltdown just by reminding yourself of what you have at stake.

The third stage of your cycle is when you give in to your impulses and you start to drink. Initially, you feel great. But after a glass or two, you have to decide if you'll stay within your drink limit and stop or continue drinking and get toasted. How do you want to feel in the morning? Terrific or terrible? The choice is obvious. There's still time to stop this runaway train!

If you take control of alcohol, stop at your limit and wake up the next morning feeling good and feeling good about yourself, congratulations! You took charge of your drinking and defeated your drinking cycle.

If you didn't take control of alcohol, drank heavily and wake up the next morning feeling like a wreck - physically and psychologically - poor you! You let booze take charge and let your cycle steamroll right over you.

You can stop your binge or problem drinking cycle at any stage. Just think of all of your opportunities to interrupt and defeat your drinking cycle before and during drinking. What will you do the next time you're confronted by your drinking cycle?

Binge or Problem Drinking Cycle Stages

1. *The perfect storm of drinking cues gathers*
2. *Drinking thinking takes over encouraging you to drink*
3. *You give in to your impulses and start drinking*
4. *You drink*
5. *You either stop at your limit or you continue to drink*

Teaser

What are your drinking cues? What's your perfect storm of drinking cues? How will you handle each one, so they don't lead to problem drinking? How will you interrupt your binge or problem drinking cycle? Record your plans.

Chapter Twelve:
Do Stress, Depression or Anxiety Trigger Your Drinking? Deal with Them!

Stress, depression and anxiety are caused by people, situations or predicaments you feel you have no control over. Unfortunately, these negative moods make alcohol and its effects more attractive to you.

Here you'll dig deeper and identify the feelings that may be affecting you, your quality of life and your drinking. Then you'll learn healthy ways to handle them, instead of hitting the bottle. In the long run, you'll be happier and you'll reduce your alcohol consumption. Payoffs!

The Top Six Reasons Why You May Become Stressed, Depressed or Anxious

School, family problems, relationships, peer pressure, low self-esteem and assuming more adult responsibilities are the top six reasons why young people get stressed, depressed or anxious. Worry about your future, money problems, holiday stress, chronic illness and being over stimulated by too many electronic devices may also factor into your feelings.

You do have a choice about how to deal with the moods and issues that drive you to drink. You can manage them in healthy ways - facing them head-on without resorting to harmful substances or behaviors. Or you can manage them in unhealthy ways - stuffing them with drugs, alcohol or destructive habits. Naturally, you want to deal with them in healthy ways so you can live a long, healthy, happy life and make your mark in the world.

Does Stress Trigger Your Drinking?

Teen and young adult years can be some of the most stressful years in your life. In fact, research shows that a third of all teenagers suffer from at least one stress-related episode every week!

What are the signs you might be stressed out? Trying to be perfect all the time - physically, academically, athletically and socially - and feeling disappointed if you think you don't measure up. Constantly feeling pressured and thinking you have too much to do. Being unable to relax and unwind, even after you've fulfilled your obligations. Not enjoying people and activities you use to enjoy. Feeling tired, down or on edge much of the time. Having trouble sleeping or eating. Having headaches or stomachaches. Feeling angry and wanting to be left alone. Being preoccupied with trying to live up to the expectations you set for yourself. Being preoccupied with trying to live up to your friend's expectations. Being preoccupied with trying to live up to your parent's expectations. Feeling overloaded and over stimulated in general. If you're suffering from any of these symptoms, you might be stressed out.

Girls seem to be more affected by stress than guys and try to reduce or eliminate it by specifically addressing it or seeking help from others. Guys, on the other hand, respond to stress by not dealing with it or the source of it. And even though most people, regardless of age, have the same types of stress responses, the issues causing the stress - the stressors - are different for young people than those for adults.

When you're young, everything in your life seems to be changing. You're going through puberty and your body is transforming from a child to an adult - hormones are surging, you're gaining weight, you're getting taller and you're maturing sexually. Guy's voices are deepening and girls are starting their periods.

You're experiencing psychological changes too. You're determined to be free, independent and on your own - not so attached to your parents and family. You're becoming more interested in sex and find yourself attracted to others. And at times you feel more impulsive, assertive and aggressive. You're also seeking out exhilarating new experiences and becoming curious about drugs and alcohol.

As if physical and psychological changes weren't enough, you may also be facing school and family challenges as well. School is becoming more demanding and doing well so you can get into a good college may be your number one priority right now. Getting good grades is one of the biggest stressors for young people today.

Your family may be a big stressor too. Asserting your independence, while you're still living at home and being supported by your parents, can be difficult and filled with conflict. It can be even harder if your parents are separated, divorced or remarried and you live in a blended family. And your stress load increases if you move or change schools because of a changing family situation.

Relationships with friends, romantic relationships and peer pressure are also probably on your stressor list. Friends - making new ones and keeping old ones - is always a big concern. And feeling you're liked and you belong is more important to you than ever. When things aren't going well socially, things aren't going well in general for most young people.

You're new to the world of sex and romantic relationships too and you're learning as you go along. Initiating a relationship, maintaining it, breaking up and getting back together again can take a toll on you. And your stress mounts.

Let's not forget that low self-esteem may also factor into your stress level. If you don't feel good about yourself and think you don't measure up, you're responsible for stressing yourself out! It's bad enough you have to compete with others when it comes to looks, school, popularity and sports, but when you set such high standards for yourself that you have a hard time living up to them, you're setting yourself up for low-self-esteem and alcohol problems.

And you're expected to assume more adult responsibilities too. If you want the freedom and independence of being an adult, you have to start acting like one and fulfilling more personal and financial obligations. You're now expected to make your own way in the world and take care of yourself. What will you do? Where will you live? How will you pay the bills? Will you get married? Will you have children? Big issues and decisions that could affect you for the rest of your life - just adding to your stress load.

Money problems, chronic illness, the death of a loved one, holiday stress and being over stimulated by too much information may also be weighing on you. In fact, you never have a quiet moment when you're not bombarded with some kind of information - compounding your stress.

You don't have to suffer from all of these symptoms to be stressed out. Just one or two can put you over the top, weigh you down and lead to problem drinking. And FYI - stress may not only lead to alcohol abuse, it may also lead to other substance abuse and behavioral problems - depression, anxiety, drug abuse, eating disorders, cutting, etc.

What stresses you out? School, family problems, relationships with friends, romantic relationships, peer pressure, low self-esteem, assuming more adult responsibilities, your future, money problems, being over stimulated by electronic devices? Know your stressors, know yourself.

Symptoms of Stress

- *You're always trying to achieve and maintain perfection*
- *You feel like you don't measure up*
- *You constantly feel pressured*
- *You're always thinking you have too much to do*
- *You're unable to relax after you fulfill your obligations*
- *You're unable to enjoy people or activities*
- *You often feel tired or down*
- *You feel on edge*
- *You have problems sleeping and/or eating*
- *You have headaches and/or stomachaches*
- *You feel angry*
- *You want to be alone*
- *You're preoccupied with living up to the expectations you set for yourself*
- *You're preoccupied with living up to the expectations of others*
- *You feel overloaded and over stimulated in general*

Tips to Manage and Overcome Stress

You can deal with stress in healthy or unhealthy ways. You can exercise to blow off steam or you can binge. You can meditate to put oversized problems in perspective or you can take out your feelings on people around you. You can practice relaxation exercises to settle down or you can gorge yourself on potato chips. Decide right now you'll deal with your stress in healthy ways, not with alcohol or other substances or activities that will harm you.

The first thing you should do so you come out on top, not the stress? Be aware of it and the role it plays in your life. Acknowledge the stress symptoms you're having, instead of ignoring them or stuffing them. You can't change what you don't acknowledge!

Once you sensitize yourself to the stress and its symptoms, look at the issues causing it - the stressors. What's going on in your life that's stressing you out? Think about it. Be clear and specific about what's weighing on you. After you've pinpointed your stressors, then you can take steps to resolve them.

You can lighten up by taking care of yourself too. Stress takes a physical toll on you and if you take good care of your body, you can help it recover. Eat right. Fill up on lots of fruits, vegetables and whole grains. Get your calcium and protein with dairy products and lean meat and fish. Avoid sweets and high-fat, high-calorie junk food. Limit caffeine. Don't smoke. And remember - alcohol and drugs will just exacerbate your pressure problem, not fix it.

Get plenty of rest. Squeeze in at least seven hours a night. Go to bed earlier and get up later, if possible. A good night's rest will relax you, energize you and reduce your stress level.

Exercise! Exercise is one of the most effective weapons in fighting stress. You'll feel better, physically and mentally, when you get out and get moving. Try to get involved in activities you really enjoy. And mix it up. Play softball one day, tennis the next. Take a brisk thirty-minute walk, if you're on your own. Go to the gym. Swim. Jog. Ride your bike. Make a point of getting at least thirty minutes of vigorous exercise every day and you'll reduce your stress level in a hurry.

Think highly of yourself. Strong self-esteem and self-confidence will help you cope with stress and its unpleasant side effects. When you think you're hot, you're more confident and you can handle pressure better. So when the going gets tough, remind yourself of how wonderful you are and that you have the ability to deal with any stressor or stressful situation. You'll see yourself through because you're the greatest!

Give yourself an attitude adjustment too. Don't set unrealistically high expectations for yourself. And cultivate a practical, positive attitude about life by putting your stressors in perspective and understanding there are some people, circumstances and events that are simply beyond your control. Also avoid highly stressful tasks and if you can't avoid them, brainstorm different ways to manage them so they aren't so stressful. Keep your head, take a step back and do your best. You'll reduce your stress load with that attitude.

Maintain a great sense of humor. Laughing at yourself and your stressors might take some weight off your shoulders. Try to find the humor in any situation and you'll laugh your tension away.

Try doing things differently as well. Prioritize and get the most important tasks of your day done first. Also give yourself plenty of time to finish tasks so you don't feel rushed. In other words, give yourself a week to write your English essay, instead of waiting until the night before. Prioritize and give yourself lots of time to get things done and you'll feel more and more relaxed.

Communicate clearly and learn to say no to people who stress you out and to obligations you don't have time for. And stand up to the notions that you have to do more and more stuff and you have to keep busy every second of the day. You don't. Just say no and you'll decrease your stress level without even trying.

Look into relaxation exercises and techniques to loosen up. Deep breathing or progressive muscle relaxation might work for you. Or listening to your favorite music, relaxation or hypnosis CDs would. Meditation, yoga, tai-chi and biofeedback have all been shown to take the pressure off. Guided imagery and visualization techniques - envisioning yourself in a fabulous setting and learning how to relax - might also give you the mini-vacation you need to unwind.

Have fun and make time for hobbies, interests and activities you enjoy. Playing and having fun is the number one antidote to stress. Draw, play with your dog, dance, bake a cake, act goofy. You forget about your troubles when you have fun.

Investigate specific stress-reduction strategies and techniques. Surf the net and go to the library to learn about different ways to deal with physical and psychological stress. Then follow through with the best ideas. You might stress less.

Cultivate a spiritual practice. Devoting time to something bigger than yourself might ease the pressure. It can be organized - a traditional religion or place of worship. Or unorganized - meditation, nature walks or good works. Think about it.

Talk to a trustworthy friend, an understanding parent or your school counselor about your stress and what's causing it, if you have the luxury of doing so. They might just offer you a different perspective that could be helpful. A little thoughtful listening and understanding might also de-stress you.

Finally, consider getting help from a mental health professional who specializes in stress reduction and management. The earlier you seek treatment, the better your chances of recovering from stress are.

Above all, don't rely on drugs, alcohol or any other potentially dangerous or addictive substance or activity to relieve stress. If you harm yourself or become addicted to an unhealthy substance or activity, you'll just be adding to your stress level.

Are you stressed out? How will you handle your stress? What healthy options will you look into to take the pressure off?

Tips to Manage and Overcome Stress

- *Become aware of stress and stress symptoms*
- *Become aware of and address the issues causing stress*
- *Eat healthy*
- *Get plenty of rest*
- *Exercise*
- *Pump up your self-esteem and self-confidence*
- *Set realistic expectations for yourself*
- *Nurture a positive, practical attitude about living*
- *Realize some circumstances are beyond your control*
- *Step back and put stressors in perspective*
- *Laugh at stress and stressors*
- *Prioritize*
- *Give yourself plenty of time to get things done*
- *Communicate clearly and assertively*
- *Learn to say no to some people and obligations*
- *Learn relaxation exercises and techniques*
- *Make time for fun activities*

- *Investigate stress reduction strategies and techniques*
- *Cultivate a spiritual practice*
- *Talk to someone you trust about your stress*
- *Talk to a mental health professional specializing in stress*
- *Seek professional help early*

Does Depression Trigger Your Drinking?

Depression in young people is a lot more common than it use to be. Today, one out of eight teenagers suffers from it. It tends to run in families and usually starts between the ages of fifteen and thirty. Depression comes and goes for most teenagers and young people, but once you experience a bout of depression you're more likely to have it again.

Depression can also trigger problem drinking. When you feel blue, you turn to booze to brighten up. In addition to alcohol abuse, depression can also lead to other self-destructive behaviors like drug abuse, eating disorders, cutting yourself and suicide.

What are the symptoms of depression? If you feel sad, unhappy, irritable, hopeless or you just don't care about life most of the time, you're depressed. If you have no energy or interest in living, you're depressed. If you no longer enjoy friends, family or activities you use to enjoy, you may be depressed. If you're getting in trouble with your parents, at school or with the law, you may be suffering from depression.

Other signs of depression may include feeling tired all the time and getting more headaches, stomachaches or backaches than usual. If you can't sleep or you're sleeping too much, if you're not eating or you're eating too much, depression might be to blame. If you have difficulty concentrating or making decisions, you may be suffering from depression. If you feel anxious and guilty and you're preoccupied with death and dying, depression could be the culprit. And if you're rebellious, promiscuous and acting irresponsibly, like using drugs, skipping school, not studying or not fulfilling obligations, depression could be the reason. Take note it's normal to feel down sometimes, but if you feel down for more than two weeks and can't shake it, you're suffering from depression.

What issues could be causing your depression? There are lots of problems that could lead to depression. Low self-esteem and thinking you're inadequate because you're too fat or your grades aren't up to par. Not having good friends or a social life. Or the trials and tribulations of a romantic relationship.

Maybe you're depressed because you moved or switched schools or you're adjusting to a new blended family living arrangement. Or because you live in a one-parent home and you're expected to assume more family and financial responsibilities than you can handle.

Maybe your depression stems from financial problems - you're unable to afford college and have to work full-time instead. Maybe you hate your job. Or you're frustrated because you can't pursue your dreams for one reason or another. Your sexual orientation - being gay - and all of the pressures that being gay entails, could also be behind your depression.

Binge or problem drinking can also be a symptom of depression. The euphoric effect of a couple of beers can be uplifting. But you might learn to rely on alcohol and develop a drinking problem. That's why it's so important to address depression early on. The sooner you whip depression, the sooner you'll whip a growing drinking problem.

Keep in mind, you don't have to suffer from all of these symptoms to be depressed. If you suffer from just one or two, you're probably suffering from depression and should do something about it.

Are you depressed? What are your symptoms? What's causing your depression? The smarter you are about depression and how to handle it, the less you'll be attracted to alcohol.

<u>Symptoms of Depression</u>

- *You feel sad, unhappy or irritable*
- *You feel hopeless about life*
- *You have no energy or interest in living*
- *You no longer enjoy family, friends or activities you use to enjoy*
- *You're getting in trouble with parents, at school, the law*
- *You feel tired often*
- *You have headaches, stomachaches or backaches often*
- *You can't sleep or you sleep too much*
- *You don't eat or you eat too much*
- *You are unable to concentrate*
- *You are unable to make decisions*
- *You feel anxious and guilty often*
- *You are preoccupied with death and dying*
- *You are rebellious, promiscuous or act irresponsibly*
- *Your depression symptoms last for more than two weeks*

Tips to Manage and Overcome Depression

If you think you suffer from depression, you could continue to feel sad and unhappy most of the time, binge and engage in other dangerous behaviors that will get you in trouble. Or you can admit you're depressed, be proactive and start doing something about it, so it doesn't lead to other problems. The choice is obvious.

Acknowledging you suffer from depression is the first step to overcoming it. You're facing the enemy head on and taking action. And taking action always feels better than just sitting back and letting depression have its way with you.

Sorting out the reasons behind your depression is the next step to healing it. And once you've identified the reasons causing your depression, it's up to you to tackle them. Brainstorm and research ways to deal with these issues constructively. Then follow through with practical solutions. Resolving the problems causing your depression will automatically elevate your mood.

Taking good care of yourself physically is also a must to break out of depression. Nutritious eating, lots of exercise and plenty of sleep improves your mood naturally. A healthy lifestyle is a great starting point to beat the blues.

Exercise! Exercise cannot be overemphasized when it comes to deflating depression. It will help you to replace your hopeless, negative feelings with positive, optimistic ones. In fact, working out on a regular basis has been proven to be just as effective as prescription antidepressants in relieving depression. Wouldn't you rather take a walk to feel better than pop a pill? Exercise works. Do it!

If you don't feel good about yourself and low self-esteem is one of the reasons behind your depression, stop putting yourself down. Make a list of all of your positive qualities and take pride in the things you do well. Don't dwell on your shortcomings and don't be so hard on yourself. Research shows the more you like yourself and nurture your self-esteem, the sooner your depression will lift.

If school is getting you down, talk to your teachers and the school counselor about your grades and how you can improve them. With a little help and effort on your part, you'll probably improve your school performance and get better grades. Or you can learn to live with average grades and still be happy. We can't all be brain surgeons.

If your friends, a romantic relationship or your social life leave a lot to be desired, re-evaluate your connections. Keep company with people who like you - not your money, not your looks and not your alcohol consumption. Stick with interesting, trustworthy people you can depend on and distance yourself from the others.

Maybe you're depressed because of family problems - your parents splitting, living with mom one week and dad the next, living in a blended family. Be patient and kind to yourself during this difficult time. You'll probably feel better eventually, but if you don't suggest family counseling to your parents to ease the pain.

If money is the source of your depression, get a job. Part-time while you're in school wouldn't hurt. You'd be a little richer, a little busier and have less time on your hands to feel blue. Or look for a better paying job, if you already work full-time. Or simplify your life and be satisfied with less. You don't want a silly thing like money to make you unhappy.

If you feel frustrated because you can't go to college or travel around the world, remember, where there's a will, there's a way. Think long-term, make a plan and plot out every step that will get you a little closer to your dream. Achieving your goals might not happen overnight, but they will happen with planning, patience, determination and following through with your long-term plan.

And if you're grappling with your sexual orientation, talk to a trusted friend, see a mental health professional or get into a support group for young people in the same boat. Once you accept and like yourself for who you are, you can come out of the closet and leave your depression behind.

Talking to a good friend or an understanding parent about your depression would be great, if you felt comfortable doing so. But if you don't have the luxury of a confidante, perhaps professional help would be the answer - helping you to sort out your feelings and getting them off your chest. Talking to a licensed mental health professional who specializes in depression might give you a whole new perspective on what's making you sad and you'd get the treatment you need to relieve it.

Do things you like to do. Little things, like having an ice cream cone, soaking in a hot tub, going to the beach or doing something nice for someone else, would be good therapy. Or big things, like taking a trip to Mexico or buying a new car. Do something fun and you won't think about how depressed you are.

Get creative. Sing, write, play an instrument, dance, draw, paint, cook, build, perform. Get involved too. Volunteer for an organization you believe in. Keep busy and you'll forget your troubles.

Look into meditation or yoga to brighten up. Mind/body practices might take your mind off your worries and increase your feelings of well being. Many people swear by them. Give one a try and see if it takes you higher.

More ideas to ease your depression? Explore alternative medicine. Splurge and get a massage. Aromatherapy might perk you up. Acupuncture has relieved depression in some people. And chiropractic treatment has also helped some people.

A few natural herbs have proven to be useful in restoring a positive outlook. St. John's Wort has been studied extensively and has been clinically proven to alleviate mild to moderate depression. Check with your physician before trying any herbal remedy because it may interact with other medications you may be taking and/or it may lead to or exacerbate a physical or psychological condition.

And if you're not sure if depression is to blame for your negative feelings, talk to your family physician, school counselor or a mental health professional. They'll interview you and may give you some psychological tests to see if depression is the reason you feel so down. Then they'll set a course of action for you to feel better.

If you really feel sad or even suicidal, run, don't walk, to the nearest psychologist, psychiatrist or mental health professional who specializes in depression. They may prescribe pharmaceutical antidepressants in addition to psychotherapy - a powerful combination to beat the blues and feel good again. In treatment, you'll start to understand the emotions, behaviors, events or problems that contribute to your depression and you'll learn how to cope with them, so you can regain some sense of control and pleasure in your life. Best to end this unhappy chapter in your life and get on with the business of living with professional help, if nothing else works for you.

If you're depressed, what will you do to improve your mood and make your life more enjoyable? Think about all of your options, then get busy and follow through with the best ones. You'll be happier, healthier and less inclined to drink.

<u>*Tips to Manage and Overcome Depression*</u>

- *Acknowledge you're depressed*
- *Address the reasons behind your depression*
- *Eat well*
- *Get plenty of rest*
- *Exercise*
- *Nurture your self-esteem*
- *Talk about your feelings*
- *Get help with school*
- *Rethink your relationships*
- *Address family problems*
- *Address money problems*
- *Acknowledge your sexual orientation*
- *Talk to a trusted friend about your feelings*
- *Do things you enjoy doing and have fun*
- *Get creative*
- *Get involved*
- *Get into a mind/body practice*
- *Explore alternative medicine remedies*
- *Seek help from a mental health professional specializing in depression*
- *Consider prescription medication*

Does Anxiety Trigger Your Drinking?

Thirteen percent of teens in this country struggle with anxiety. In most cases, anxiety begins and continues because you have an unrealistic view of your problems. You exaggerate them in your mind, you stress out and you become anxious. In fact, anxiety is a normal reaction to stress and it often starts in childhood or adolescence.

More women suffer from generalized anxiety disorder than men. And if you experience generalized anxiety, you may also suffer from other anxiety disorders, like panic attacks, phobias, obsessive-compulsive disorders and drug abuse. Anxiety can also trigger binge or problem drinking.

What are the symptoms of anxiety? If you feel nervous, worry about every little thing for no good reason and you can't stop worrying about school, family, friends, money or your health, you're suffering from anxiety. If you worry too much about everyday events and activities and you're always double-checking to make sure you did the right thing, you're experiencing anxiety. If you feel panicky when things aren't going well or when you're in a stressful situation, you're anxious. If your worries are unrealistic or out of proportion to the situation at hand, you're suffering from anxiety. If you feel fearful to the point that it interferes with your daily functioning, you're experiencing anxiety.

Constant, excessive worry and tension are the most obvious signs of anxiety. You know, that nervous, jittery, edgy feeling you get when you're worried about something. Other symptoms may include irritability, difficulty concentrating, fatigue, restlessness, headaches, muscle tension, trouble sleeping, trouble eating, sweating, trembling, going to the bathroom frequently and being easily startled. And you don't have to have all of these symptoms to be considered anxious. Just one or two symptoms are enough.

What causes anxiety? Even though the exact cause of anxiety is unknown, genetics, brain chemistry and environmental stresses are all thought to play a role in developing it. Research suggests anxiety runs in families. That is, if you have family members who suffer from it, you're more likely to suffer from it. Genes may cause anxiety in some people.

If you have abnormal levels of specific neurotransmitters in your brain, you're also more likely to have an anxiety disorder. Neuro-transmitters are chemical messengers in your brain that move information between nerve cells and when they're out of balance, messages can't be processed through your brain properly. This alters the way your brain reacts and can lead to anxiety.

Environmental factors may also cause anxiety. Stressful events, such as moving away from home, changing schools or jobs, relationship problems, coming out, divorce or the death of a loved one, can all trigger anxiety.

Anxiety often worsens when you're stressed about something and it can lead to an increased use of addictive substances, like alcohol, drugs, caffeine and nicotine. Yes, liquor may mellow you out temporarily. But if you drink too much, it can actually have the opposite effect. It can increase your anxiety.

Do you suffer from anxiety? What are your symptoms? Is there a history of anxiety in your family? Did a stressful event or situation cause your anxious feelings? The more you know, the less anxious you'll be and the less you'll lean on alcohol to calm down.

<u>Symptoms of Anxiety</u>

- *Constant excessive worry, tension and nervousness*
- *You can't stop worrying*
- *You worry for no good reason*
- *You worry about everyday activities*
- *You feel panicky when you're stressed*
- *Your worry is unrealistic or out of proportion*
- *You feel fearful often*
- *Anxiety dominates your thinking*
- *You're irritable*
- *You have difficulty concentrating*
- *You suffer from fatigue*
- *You suffer from restlessness*
- *You suffer from headaches and muscle tension*
- *You have trouble eating or sleeping*
- *You sweat or tremble*
- *You go to the bathroom frequently*
- *You're easily startled*

Tips to Manage and Overcome Anxiety

Some people handle anxiety in unhealthy ways - with alcohol, drugs, cigarettes or food - and never really fix the problem. But if you deal with it in healthy ways, you'll feel calmer and more relaxed in general and you won't develop substance abuse problems. Healthy ways are the ways to go.

If you're anxious, try to figure out what's causing it. Are you lacking in self-esteem and self-confidence? Don't know a soul in your new school? Won't graduate unless you pass the science final? Coping with a new blended family? Still waiting to be accepted to college? Are you stretched thin between home, school and your job? Think about what's causing the fear and worry and take it from there.

After you identify the issues making you nervous, put together a plan to resolve them. And if you can't eliminate or limit the problems, change your attitude about them. Put them in perspective and focus on everything else that's going right in your life. Be patient and keep plugging away. Hopefully, you'll feel better once you become aware of the anxiety-provoking issues and take steps to fix them.

A healthy lifestyle will step on anxiety naturally. Good food, no junk. Plenty of rest. Lots of exercise. And avoiding caffeine in coffee, tea and soda will settle you down.

Talking about your anxiety and what's behind it can also relieve it. Perhaps a friend, family member, your physician or clergyman can help. Talking about your feelings with someone you trust may be all you need to relax.

Work on your mindset too. If worrying about people, relationships, events and circumstances beyond your control drives you crazy, try to accept them and move on. Some things you just can't change, but you can change your mind and the way you think about certain things. Changing your mind about problems might be easier than trying to change the problems themselves.

Challenge negative thinking that makes you nervous too. Whenever your mind wanders to those dark, anxiety-provoking places stop yourself and replace those negative thoughts with positive ones. You'll feel less anxious. You can control how you think and feel. Anxiety is truly a mind game.

You can also employ many of the same relaxation strategies and techniques useful in managing stress and depression. Meditation, deep breathing and relaxation CDs have all been proven to reduce anxiety. Guided imagery, visualization and acupuncture may be helpful too. And listening to calming music and practicing yoga could be valuable tools in your anxiety-reducing toolbox. Learn to relax and you can't be anxious!

Biofeedback might resolve your anxiety. Biofeedback is based on the idea that when you are given information about your body's physiological processes, you can use this information to control them. Specifically, if you become aware of your body's physiological responses to anxiety, you can control these responses and control your anxiety. Biofeedback uses electronic instruments to measure your physiological responses when you feel anxious, then, with the help of a therapist, you learn how to relax and you lessen your anxiety.

Hypnosis or hypnotherapy may also be useful in fighting anxiety. One or the other could help you to expose painful thoughts, feelings and memories that are causing your nervousness. And they might help you to perceive people, situations and things differently and give you suggestions on how to manage or eliminate anxiety or the source of your anxiety.

Psychotherapy is another avenue you should explore to put your anxiety to rest. Identifying people or events that trigger your anxiety and learning healthy ways to cope with them will reduce your worry and enable you to get on with your healthy, happy life. Your therapist will interview you and may give you a psychological test or two to determine if you're anxious. Then they'll draw up a treatment plan for you and you'll be on the road to recovery.

Alternative nutritional and herbal remedies have also been used to treat anxiety. Again, talk to your doctor if you're considering taking any nutritional or herbal supplement. They may interact with other medications you may be taking or cause or exacerbate a physical or psychological condition.

If all else fails, there are a number of prescription medications on the market that target anxiety. Talk to your doctor or a mental health professional to see if you'd be a good candidate for anxiety medication.

How can you reduce the anxiety in your life? What healthy options will you follow through with to calm down? Don't worry, be happy.

Tips to Manage and Overcome Anxiety

- *Identify the issues causing anxiety*
- *Address the issues causing anxiety*
- *Eat well*
- *Get plenty of rest*
- *Exercise*
- *Avoid caffeine in coffee, tea or soda*
- *Talk about your feelings*
- *Change your mindset about the issues causing anxiety*
- *Challenge anxiety-provoking thinking*
- *Practice relaxation strategies and techniques*
- *Listen to calming music*
- *Practice biofeedback techniques*
- *Try hypnosis or hypnotherapy*
- *Consider psychotherapy*
- *Consider herbal or nutritional supplements*
- *Consider prescription medication*

Teaser

Do you suffer from stress, depression and/or anxiety? How do they affect your drinking? Do you drink more? Put together plans to reduce your stress, depression and/or anxiety if they trip your desire to drink and problem drinking. Then put them to work and feel better!

Chapter Thirteen:
Do You Hold Mistaken Beliefs, Expectations and Myths About Drinking and Alcohol? Toss Them!

Is your mind cluttered with untrue, unhealthy and unrealistic notions about drinking and alcohol that help you rationalize your drinking? If it is, it's time to separate fact from fiction and clean up the clutter. The more realistic you are about what booze can or can't do for you, the less inclined you'll be to use it or abuse it.

First, Toss False Beliefs About Drinking and Alcohol

Like it or not, you've picked up conscious and subconscious beliefs about drinking and alcohol from your friends and family that haunt you to this day. You learned alcohol use or abuse was good or bad, healthy or unhealthy.

Research shows positive beliefs about liquor and its effects are established early in life. You probably viewed booze and drinking as bad before you were nine. But by the age of thirteen, you saw spirits in a better light. And unfortunately, the more positive your beliefs about alcohol, the earlier you start to drink, the more you drink and the more often you drink.

What positive beliefs about drinking and alcohol have you been raised with? Which ones are true? Which ones aren't? If you corrected your false beliefs about booze, you could no longer lean on them as excuses to drink and you'd reduce your alcohol consumption.

First, look at notions you picked up from your family. Start by looking at your family's history of alcohol use. Did you come from a family of teetotalers? No liquor was kept in the house and drinking was frowned upon? You learned alcohol and drinking were unacceptable.

Were your parents moderate drinkers? Would they drink a couple of times a week with dinner or when they were going out? A cocktail was a treat, but never the focus. They never had any problems with the bottle and they never got drunk. You learned alcohol was just a nice complement to life - nothing more.

Or were they an abusive lot who drank frequently or drank heavily or got drunk often? Did they drink everyday? Was beer, wine or hard liquor the highlight of their day? Did they drink until they were drunk? Did they drink for no good reason? Was any occasion a drinking occasion? Or were they binge drinkers who didn't drink that often, but when they did they got smashed? Consequently, you learned from their example that every day is a drinking day, every occasion is a drinking occasion and every time you drink, you get toasted.

Now look at the beliefs about drinking and alcohol you picked up from friends. Were you with pals when you took your first nip? What were the circumstances? Did you and your friends drink for fun, to socialize, to rebel, to kill time or for all of the above reasons? Was drinking a way to make friends and a must to party? Did you and your buddies binge and get drunk most every time you drank? You learned booze was essential to socializing, fitting in, rebelling and entertaining yourself. And when you drink, you drink to get drunk.

If you were blessed with moderate drinking role models and you learned healthy, realistic attitudes about drinking and alcohol, lucky you. But if you grew up with alcohol abusing role models and you learned unhealthy, unrealistic attitudes about booze that encourage your problem drinking, it's time to correct your beliefs and behavior.

A healthy, realistic set of beliefs about drinking and alcohol starts with thinking that drinking is acceptable only under certain circumstances. It's appropriate if you're eating, socializing or celebrating. And it's moderate drinking - only a drink or two per occasion. It's pacing your drinking - not guzzling or bingeing. It's knowing a couple of cocktails can enhance the quality of your life, but more won't. You never rely on liquor to cope with feelings or moods. You never use it to entertain yourself because you're lonely or bored. And you never use it just to pass the time. It's never the focus of the party, the day or your life. And you never - ever - get drunk.

An unhealthy, unrealistic set of beliefs about drinking and alcohol, on the other hand, starts with thinking it's acceptable anytime, anywhere and for any reason. Any occasion is a drinking occasion. Drinking as much and as fast as you can is acceptable. Drinking to get drunk is fun and acceptable. Mindless drinking in front of the TV every night is okay. Getting smashed every Friday or Saturday night or every weekend, all weekend, is okay. Having four or five drinks every day, regardless of your schedule, is okay. Beer is a prescription for a bad day. Liquor is good medicine for any feeling or mood. Drinking at home alone, when you're lonely or bored, is an acceptable way to kill time. Drinking when you have something important to do, like going to work or school, is acceptable. Booze is the focus of the party, the day and your life. And getting drunk often is acceptable.

What are your beliefs about drinking and alcohol? Who did you pick them up from? Which ones rationalize or encourage your binge or problem drinking? Toss them.

<u>Healthy, Realistic Beliefs About Drinking and Alcohol</u>

- *Drinking is acceptable only under certain circumstances*
- *Drinking is appropriate when you're eating, socializing or celebrating*
- *Moderate drinking - nothing more - will enhance the quality of your life*
- *You never rely on alcohol to cope with feelings or moods*
- *You never rely on alcohol to entertain yourself when you're bored or lonely*
- *You never use alcohol just to pass the time*
- *Alcohol is never the focus of the party, the day or your life*
- *Getting drunk - ever - is totally unacceptable*

<u>Unhealthy, Unrealistic Beliefs About Drinking and Alcohol</u>

- *Drinking is acceptable anytime, anywhere, for any reason*
- *Any occasion is a drinking occasion*
- *Drinking as much and as fast as you can is acceptable*
- *Drinking to get drunk is fun and acceptable*
- *Chronic heavy drinking is acceptable*
- *Drinking to cope with feelings and moods is acceptable*
- *Drinking is a good way to entertain yourself or pass the time*
- *Drinking when you have important obligations to fulfill is acceptable*
- *Alcohol is the focus of the party, the day and your life*
- *Getting drunk often is acceptable*

Second, Toss False Expectations About Drinking and Alcohol

Expectations about booze you've picked up from others, just like learned beliefs, can also shape your drinking behavior and encourage problem drinking. Do you expect to have fun when you drink? Do you expect to feel better when you drink? Do you expect alcohol to put you at ease in social situations? Do you expect beer to help you fit in and make friends? Do you expect to feel more attractive and sexier when you're under the influence? Do you expect to feel better about yourself when you get high? Do you expect to feel more confident too? Do you think liquor is an excellent remedy for stress, depression, anxiety or any other negative feelings? Figure out what you expect from alcohol, eliminate your unhealthy, unrealistic expectations about it and you'll be less inclined to abuse it.

It's true, drinking in moderation - a cocktail or two - will improve your mood and may make you feel better. It's relaxing and reduces stress and tension. A drink or two might actually be good for you, physically and mentally. A great case for smart drinking.

But thinking that more booze is better and the more you drink, the better you'll feel, is a mistake many drinkers make. It's just not true. More than a couple of drinks and your body and brain become impaired, you get drunk, you blackout and have a hangover the next morning. Anything more than smart drinking - more than a drink or two - backfires on you. Don't get caught up in the "more is better" trap.

And social situations do seem easier to handle when you're under the influence of beer. The social anxiety you feel about meeting new people and making friends melts away after a bottle or two. Yes, booze in moderation is an effective social lubricant.

But when you go beyond moderation, you become less inhibited. You also become more verbal, impulsive and aggressive and say and do things you'd never dream of saying or doing if you were sober or just mildly high. You become offensive and the party isn't fun anymore. The polite behavior associated with moderate drinking evaporates and all you remember the next day is getting drunk and behaving badly.

And if you think alcohol is good for building and maintaining relationships, think again. Liquor, most often, has the opposite effect. Too much of it destroys relationships. When you overdo it, you're likely to become rude or sloppy or mean or unreliable. Qualities that drive people away from you, instead of drawing them to you.

153

If you expect beer to take the pressure out of peer pressure, you're fooling yourself. Are you sure you want to hang with people who like you because of how many six-packs you can put away? You don't. Depending on any substance, including alcohol, to fit in doesn't work. You are your own intelligent and independent person and you don't have to mindlessly do what everyone else is doing - like bingeing and getting drunk - to make friends and have a social life. Just be true to yourself and you'll fit in and be popular with people who truly value and respect you. People just like you! So much for fitting in with beer.

Maybe one or two cocktails will enhance your self-esteem - short-term. But thinking that drinking will increase your self-worth permanently is crazy. And if you go over your limit, it's a different story altogether. You're hung over, you may be embarrassed about what you said or did and you're ashamed of yourself. And your self-worth and reputation are in shreds. Think about it. Out-of-control drinking is really a self-esteem buster, not an enhancer.

You might think a couple of shots will increase your self-confidence too. And you might be right. But it's an illusion that will wear off when the alcohol wears off. And bingeing actually has the opposite effect. It decreases your self-confidence. Yes, when you're drunk you think you're invincible. That self-confidence is the alcohol talking. Reality bites when you come down. Instead of feeling like conquering the world, you feel like hiding from it. Shouldn't your goal be to feel confident when you're stone cold sober? That self-confidence is real and lasts and the only way you can acquire it is through positive actions and accomplishments, not with beer.

You may think liquor will help you to deal with stress caused by big changes going on in your life. You're becoming an adult and the transition from kid to grownup can be tough - physically, psychologically, socially, intellectually and spiritually. You're also assuming more adult responsibilities - building relationships, going to college, going to work, paying bills, living independently, maybe getting married and becoming a parent. And you expect alcohol to take the edge off of this life-changing transition. But chronic, heavy drinking won't. It will, in fact, stunt your growth - physically, psychologically, socially, intellectually and spiritually - and make your transition and your life as an adult more difficult.

You may also expect alcohol to help you cope with emotional problems. Anger, frustration, loneliness, the turmoil of a romantic relationship, worry about your future. If you drink to cope with emotional problems, don't. Even moderate drinking during these tough times can be risky. You start relying on liquor more and more to see you through and pretty soon you're addicted to it. And instead of making you feeling better, heavy drinking makes you feel even worse.

Maybe you think drinking is a defiant gesture and makes you a rebel. You think it's a good way to get back at school, your parents, society, the system. Or that bingeing is an expression of your individuality. Or that you'll have exciting new experiences when you drink. Getting drunk will get you noticed - for all of the wrong reasons. And you'll probably have some really unusual - mostly negative - experiences when you get wasted. Can't you get creative and think of better ways to rebel, express yourself or have thrilling new experiences - other than getting drunk? You can.

Finally, alcohol abuse can make you sick and you can die from too much booze. No truer words were ever spoken. Expect to check out early, if you're a chronic binge drinker.

What are your expectations about alcohol? How have they shaped your drinking behavior? Which ones rationalize or encourage your binge or problem drinking? Toss the ones that drive you to drink.

Healthy, Realistic Expectations About Drinking and Alcohol

- *One or two drinks is enough to feel relaxed and happy*
- *More alcohol does not make you feel better*
- *Drinking to fit in doesn't work*
- *Alcohol does not help build or maintain healthy relationships*

- *Moderate drinking will increase your self-esteem temporarily*
- *Moderate drinking will increase your self-confidence temporarily*
- *Alcohol abuse makes you act erratically and impulsively*
- *Alcohol abuse causes or exacerbates negative feelings and moods*
- *Alcohol abuse stunts your growth*
- *Alcohol abuse ruins your reputation*
- *Alcohol abuse gets you in trouble*
- *Alcohol abuse makes you sick*
- *You can die from alcohol abuse*

Unhealthy, Unrealistic Expectations About Drinking and Alcohol

- *Alcohol will make you happier long-term*
- *The more alcohol you drink, the better you'll feel*
- *Alcohol will make you more popular*
- *Alcohol will help you build and maintain healthy relationships*
- *Drinking will relieve peer pressure*
- *Alcohol will increase your self-esteem long-term*
- *Alcohol will increase your self-confidence long-term*
- *Alcohol will resolve emotional problems long-term*
- *Drinking makes you a rebel*
- *Drinking is an expression of your individuality*
- *Drinking opens you up to exciting new experiences*

Finally, Toss Myths About Drinking and Alcohol

In addition to crazy beliefs and expectations about booze, you might also buy into these crazy myths about it too. What are your favorites?

Myth: No one in my family is an alcoholic, so I'll never be an alcoholic.

Truth: Anyone can become an alcoholic - even if you don't have a family history of alcoholism.

Myth: I get sick before I have too much to drink.

Truth: If you get sick, that's a sign you've had too much to drink!

156

Myth: I have a hollow leg and can hold my liquor.

> Truth: Tolerance is in play here. You can drink lots of alcohol without getting drunk because you've developed a high physical tolerance to it. You develop a high tolerance to spirits when you drink too much, too often. A high tolerance to alcohol is not a good thing and nothing to be proud of. It's a symptom of alcoholism.

Myth: Only sloppy drinkers become alcoholics.

> Truth: You don't have to look or act sloppy to have a drinking problem or to be an alcoholic.

Myth: I only started drinking two years ago, so I can't be an alcoholic. It takes years to become an alcoholic.

> Truth: Some people can become alcoholics within months of starting drinking.

Myth: Look at me - I'm clean and well-groomed - I can't be an alcoholic.

> Truth: Looks can be deceiving. Even if you clean up nicely, you can still be an alcoholic.

Myth: If you stick to the same kind of drink, you won't get drunk.

> Truth: If you drink too much of any one thing - beer, wine or hard liquor - you'll still get drunk.

Myth: If you drink beer all night, you won't get drunk.

> Truth: You can get drunk on just beer. Even though it has a lower alcoholic content than wine and hard liquor, if you drink enough of it you'll get wasted.

Myth: You get drunk if you switch drinks.

> Truth: Alcohol is alcohol whether it's beer, wine or vodka. If you overdo it with just one kind of drink or you overdo it with different kinds of drinks, you'll still get drunk. Switching doesn't make any difference.

Myth: Coffee or a cold shower will sober you up fast if you have to drive.

Truth: Caffeine or a cold shower will not sober you up to drive. Time is the only thing that will sober you up. You have to wait until your body has metabolized the alcohol in your system before you're capable of driving.

Myth: As long as I only drink beer and stay away from the hard stuff, I'll never become an alcoholic.

Truth: You can become alcoholic on beer and beer alone.

Myth: I've never been arrested when I was drinking or drunk, so I'm not an alcoholic.

Truth: Just because you've never been arrested when you were drinking or drunk doesn't mean you're not an alcoholic. The law catches up with only a tiny fraction of drinkers who drink and drive or break the law when they're under the influence. Even if you don't have an arrest record, you can still be an alcoholic.

Myth: My friends and I only get drunk once or twice a week. We study the rest of the time so we're not alcoholics.

Truth: Even if you're full-time students and limit your partying to once or twice a week you can still be alcoholics.

Myth: I only drink and get drunk on weekends or at parties, so I'll never be an alcoholic.

Truth: You can still be an alcoholic even if you limit your drinking to weekends and parties. You don't have to drink every day to be an alcoholic.

Myth: Drunks stay drunk all the time.

Truth: Not so. You can still be an alcoholic and have some lucid moments during the day before you start hitting the bottle.

Myth: Booze peps me up.

Truth: Maybe you feel pepped up after one or two drinks. But it's all downhill from there because alcohol is a depressant. Too much of it will eventually take you down and you'll run out of steam.

Myth: I always know when to stop drinking.

Truth: If you've had a lot to drink, you don't know when to stop drinking because you're high and your judgment is impaired.

Myth: It's safe to drive if I don't feel drunk.

Truth: Even if you don't feel drunk, alcohol impairs your reflexes, coordination and ability to make wise decisions. It's the alcohol telling you it's safe to drive!

Myth: Beer and wine are safer to drink than other liquors because they're not as strong. You can never get drunk on them.

Truth: Wrong. You just have to drink more beer or wine, compared to hard liquor, to get drunk. If you drink enough of any alcoholic beverage, you'll get drunk.

Myth: Drunks stick together. None of my friends are alcoholics, so I must not be one.

Truth: Even though you and your friends may hold down jobs or go to school, you can still be alcoholics. You don't have to be a barfly or in the gutter to be an alcoholic.

Myth: I'm confident I'll never have problems with booze, even though I party a lot.

Truth: How many young people who have been thrown in jail for drunk driving, hurt someone when they were intoxicated or didn't graduate from college because they were too busy bingeing have told themselves, "It'll never happen to me"? It happened to them and it will happen to you if you drink recklessly. You're not special.

There you have it. Myths about drinking and alcohol that might support your drinking. You can probably think of more if you put your mind to it.

What myths about drinking and alcohol do you buy into? Which ones perpetuate your problem drinking? Toss these myths and you'll run out of excuses to abuse alcohol.

Teaser

What mistaken beliefs, expectations and myths do you hold about drinking and alcohol? Identify them and record them. Then, when one passes your mind to rationalize heavy or inappropriate drinking, dismiss it. It will make a smart drinker out of you!

Chapter Fourteen:
Control Your Thinking and You'll Control Your Drinking

Change your mind and change your life. It's true. When you change your thinking about drinking, you'll change your drinking behavior too. And this is your golden opportunity to think and act differently around alcohol.

First, you'll fine tune your alcohol attitude adjustment, then you'll identify and talk back to your drinking thinking that encourages problem drinking and finally, you'll learn how to motivate yourself to stay on the smart drinking track.

The sooner you change your mind about alcohol and drinking, the sooner you'll become a smart drinker. It's that simple.

First, Fine Tune Your Alcohol Attitude Adjustment

What is an alcohol attitude adjustment? It's putting alcohol in perspective and realizing it only plays a small role in your healthy, happy life - nothing more. Booze rates low on your list of priorities and it takes a back seat to everything else - family, friends, school, work, play, fulfillment. And it's not the focus of your day or your life.

You'll know you've made your alcohol attitude adjustment when you no longer spend a lot of time thinking about drinking, drinking or recovering from the effects of drinking.

What's your payoff for making an alcohol attitude adjustment? You'll drink less naturally because it's just not that important to you. You won't feel the need to binge, get drunk or use liquor inappropriately. You'll drink smart automatically. Payoff!

How do you make your alcohol attitude adjustment? Start by thinking of the people and things that you value more than booze. Your health, your family, your friends, having fun, finishing school, traveling the world, buying a new car, graduating from college, getting a good job, having plenty of money, getting married, becoming a parent, helping others less fortunate. Living a healthy, happy, fulfilling life. These things are so much more important to you than beer and getting drunk. Everyday, give serious thought to the people and things you prize more than alcohol. You'll be minimizing the role of liquor in your life and you'll be well on your way to making your alcohol attitude adjustment.

Also remind yourself you'll have a tough time meeting your life goals if you focus on alcohol and make it the centerpiece of your life. Too much of it will keep you from leading the life you envision for yourself. You have so much more on your plate than beer. Besides, really great times happen with no booze or very little booze. Meditate on these thoughts everyday and you'll get even closer to owning your alcohol attitude adjustment.

Once these ideas sink in and they're yours, your alcohol attitude adjustment will be complete. It may take some time, so be patient with yourself. But when you have achieved the proper attitude about alcohol, your drinking behavior will reflect it and you'll drink less naturally.

Second, Identify and Talk Back to Your Drinking Thinking

Learn what drinking thinking is and how you can control it, so you master alcohol, instead of alcohol mastering you. Controlling your thinking so you drink less? It's not only possible, it's easy!

What Is Drinking Thinking?

Everyday, all day, you have a running conversation going on in your head - self-talk. In addition to thinking about your past and future, you're also thinking about your activities for the day, problems you might encounter and how you'll work through those problems. You're making decisions throughout the day and weighing the pros and cons of those decisions too.

Some self-talk may simply be deciding what to wear or what to have for lunch. Some may be deciding if you'll hang out with friends on Saturday night or if you'll go shopping in the city next week. Other thinking and self-talk may involve more serious subjects, like when you'll find time to study or how you'll wrap up loose ends at work. You have a million thoughts running through your head everyday and you're always making decisions about yourself, your lifestyle and your future.

When you think about drinking, when you're drinking and when you're thinking about stopping drinking, you're also engaging in self-talk and may fall victim to drinking thinking - a specific kind of self-talk that encourages you to drink. Drinking thinking is when you talk yourself into drinking, bingeing and getting drunk with lame excuses or faulty reasoning. It happens when you're drinking or considering drinking - whether you're aware of it or not.

The bottom line is if you're going to be a successful smart drinker, you'll have to become aware of your drinking thinking and start talking back to it - so you can prevent binge or problem drinking and stay on the moderate drinking track forever.

Prime Examples of Drinking Thinking

Sometimes your drinking thinking rationalizes drinking and getting drunk in spite of having important activities or obligations to fulfill. "I've got a test tomorrow, but who cares? I've done okay on tests when I've partied the night before." Or "I'd rather drink with my pals right now than play in the soccer game tomorrow." Or "I've handled business meetings, the boss and a hangover before and I can do it again." The "alcohol doesn't stop me from meeting my obligations" excuse.

Often, drinking thinking kicks in when you're in a bad mood. "I've had a terrible day - a beer will mellow me out." Or "I deserve a drink after that blowout with my girlfriend." Or "I'm depressed about school and my grades - a glass of wine will make me feel better." The "alcohol is medicine" excuse.

Or drinking thinking convinces you bingeing is an adventure. "I'm a party guy. Why not see how many shots it takes me to get wasted?" The "drinking alcohol is an adventure" excuse.

Drinking thinking is especially handy in social situations. "I'll feel more relaxed, have more fun and fit in at the party if I drink." The "alcohol is needed for socializing" excuse.

"Booze is legal, convenient and socially acceptable. Everybody does it." The "alcohol is an acceptable drug" excuse.

"I'm smarter, funnier and sexier when I drink. And I feel better about myself and more confident in general after a few beers." The "alcohol is a self-esteem and self-confidence booster" excuse to rationalize heavy drinking.

"I'm mad at everyone and everything, so I'm tying one on tonight." The "alcohol is a weapon" excuse - guaranteed to get you smashed.

"I deserve to get drunk - I studied for finals all week and a keg party is my payoff." The "alcohol is the payoff" excuse.

"If I feel this good after two beers, imagine what I'll feel like after ten. Fantastic!" The "more alcohol the better" excuse. Most people really believe this, especially when they're high.

"Just one more glass of wine won't hurt." The "more alcohol won't hurt" excuse. Encouraging drinking by telling yourself having more wine really won't make any difference one way or the other.

"This is such a special occasion, let's get drunk." The "alcohol makes a special occasion more special" excuse - overused by anyone who has a drinking problem. You can make a special occasion out of anything!

"I've been so good for so long, it's okay for me to get wasted." The "alcohol is my reward for not drinking" excuse that has been the downfall of many a problem drinker.

"Binge drinking is just a phase. I'll grow out of it, so I'm not going to stress about it right now." The "I'll worry about alcohol later" excuse. Useful when you need to explain away heavy drinking.

"My drinking is my own business and it doesn't hurt anyone else." The "alcohol's my business" excuse. Alcohol abuse not only has a negative impact on you, it has a negative impact on others around you too.

"I can handle my drinking without any problems." The "I control alcohol" excuse. Be clear, more than one or two drinks and you do not control alcohol, it controls you.

"Alcohol is not that harmful and there are lots of other things worse than booze. I don't do drugs." The "alcohol isn't that bad" excuse. Just because you don't do drugs doesn't make binge drinking okay. Besides, alcohol is a drug.

"I'm smarter than most people and can manage alcohol better than most people." The "I can outsmart alcohol" excuse that has brought many drinkers to their knees.

"I work hard and I play hard, so when I drink, I get smashed." The "it's okay to take alcohol to the extreme" excuse that implies if you don't get drunk, you're a wimp.

"I have to have more drinks if my friends offer them to me. It's rude to refuse them." The "I'm rude if I refuse alcohol" excuse. You have good manners if you continue to drink and get drunk?

"I'd like to cut down or stop drinking, but I can't afford it." The "affordability of alcohol treatment" excuse. Many moderate drinking and abstinence programs are free.

"I know when I've had enough, when to stop drinking and if it's safe to drive." The "I know my limits with alcohol" excuse. Many a drunk driver has used this reasoning.

"I can stop drinking anytime I want to. And I don't want to right now." The "I don't have a problem with alcohol" excuse. And denial runs rampant.

What excuses and reasons do you dream up to rationalize or encourage your drinking? The more aware you are of your drinking thinking, the less you'll fall for it.

Drinking Thinking Excuses

- *The "alcohol doesn't stop me from meeting my obligations" excuse*
- *The "alcohol is medicine" excuse*
- *The "drinking alcohol is an adventure" excuse*
- *The "alcohol is needed for socializing" excuse*
- *The "alcohol is an acceptable drug" excuse*
- *The "alcohol is a self-esteem and self-confidence booster" excuse*
- *The "alcohol is a weapon" excuse*
- *The "alcohol is the payoff" excuse*
- *The "more alcohol the better" excuse*
- *The "more alcohol won't hurt" excuse*
- *The "alcohol makes special occasions more special" excuse*
- *The "alcohol is my reward for not drinking" excuse*
- *The "I'll worry about alcohol later" excuse*
- *The "alcohol's my own business" excuse*
- *The "I can control alcohol" excuse*
- *The "alcohol isn't that bad" excuse*
- *The "I can outsmart alcohol" excuse*
- *The "it's okay to take alcohol to the extreme" excuse*
- *The "I'm rude if I refuse alcohol" excuse*

- *The "affordability of alcohol treatment" excuse*
- *The "I know my limits with alcohol" excuse*
- *The "I don't have a problem with alcohol" excuse*

How Do You Defeat Your Drinking Thinking?

Controlling your drinking thinking is really a three stage process. First, you must become aware of your thoughts - the reasons and excuses you make up to encourage your drinking. Then you must realize how ridiculous these reasons are and you poke holes in the logic behind them. And finally, you replace your illogical drinking thinking excuses that support your problem drinking with logical reasons that will your support smart drinking instead.

"I've got a test tomorrow, but who cares? I've done okay on tests when I partied the night before." Or "I'd rather drink with my pals right now than play in the soccer game tomorrow." Or "I've handled business meetings, the boss and a hangover before and I can do it again." The "alcohol doesn't stop me from meeting my obligations" excuse. You're really telling yourself beer is more important to you than school, your team or your job. Is it really? It shouldn't be. Deep down you know you'll do your best meeting important obligations if you drink moderately.

"I've had a terrible day - a beer will mellow me out." Or "I deserve a drink after that blowout with my girlfriend." Or "I'm depressed about school and my grades - a glass of wine will make me feel better." The "alcohol is medicine" excuse. No, alcohol is not medicine even though some people try to heal themselves with it. If you have emotional or mood problems, you should be looking into healthy, appropriate ways to deal with them, instead of turning to the bottle for a quick fix.

"I'm a party guy. Why not see how many shots it takes for me to get wasted?" The "drinking alcohol is an adventure" excuse. True, it's normal for young people to be curious about alcohol and its effects. But you don't have to get falling down drunk when you experiment with booze. A drink or two will allow you to experience the effects of liquor - without making yourself sick. Smart drinking makes so much sense!

"I'll feel more relaxed and have more fun at the party if I drink." The "alcohol is needed for socializing" excuse. A little liquor may take the edge off of your social anxiety when you get together with friends and strangers. The problem is when your drinking gets out of hand. When you get caught up in the moment at a party, you don't think about how much or how fast you're drinking, you drink mindlessly, it goes to your head and you get loaded. That's the problem with beer to relieve social anxiety. On the other hand, if you took smart drinking seriously - even at parties - you could lighten up a little without doing harm to yourself or anyone else.

"Booze is legal, convenient and socially acceptable. Everybody does it." The "alcohol is an acceptable drug" excuse. Just because it's legal, convenient and socially acceptable, do you have to binge and get drunk? You don't! And even though it's the drug of choice for many teens and young adults, drinking in excess is not legally or socially acceptable. Moderate drinking is legal and socially acceptable when you're twenty-one or older, but bingeing and getting drunk are not!

"I'm smarter, funnier and sexier when I drink." The "alcohol is a self-esteem and self-confidence booster" excuse. True, some alcohol can make you feel better about yourself and increase your self-confidence temporarily. But if you binge, you lose it. You stumble around, slur your words, do things you'd never dream of doing and look like an idiot. You don't look smart, funny or sexy when you're intoxicated. And as soon as you sober up, you're back to reality. Your goal should be to feel smart, funny and sexy all the time, not just when you're high. Figure that out and you might not abuse alcohol.

"I'm mad at everyone and everything so I'm tying one on tonight." The "alcohol is a weapon" excuse. Getting back at the world with booze. If getting tanked is your way of rebelling against family, school, society and the system, your plan is backfiring. You're doing more harm to yourself than anyone else. Sure, getting wasted will make you a thorn in everyone's side. But it hurts you even more. Instead of earning your diploma, traveling the world, getting a great job or earning plenty of money, you earn a bad reputation and an arrest record. Think of more creative ways to rebel. Organize, protest, get a tattoo, enroll in drama school, do something wild and crazy that doesn't hurt you or anyone else. Bingeing doesn't work. You're only shooting yourself in the foot.

"I deserve to get drunk - I studied for finals all week and a keg party is my payoff." The "alcohol is the payoff" excuse. Another seemingly logical reason to get loaded. You work hard and your reward is getting drunk. Making yourself sick, blacking out and having a hangover is your reward for acing finals? That doesn't make sense. Why not think of other less painful payoffs, like buying yourself new clothes, going to the home game, camping for the weekend or getting a massage. Think of a healthy reward - not an unhealthy one like getting polluted - when you do something right and want to do something nice for yourself.

"If I feel this good after two beers, imagine what I'll feel like after ten. Fantastic!" The "more alcohol is better" excuse to drink the night away. Most people really believe this when they're high. Obviously, it's not true for booze. Even though we're taught from an early age that more is better, this concept doesn't apply to liquor. In fact, applying it to alcohol can be deadly. The more beer you consume, the more impaired and out of it you become - physically and mentally. You could die from alcohol poisoning. Delete this drinking thinking from your brain this very minute. And repeat to yourself over and over, "more is not better when it comes to alcohol".

"Just one more glass of wine won't hurt." The "more alcohol won't hurt" excuse. Drinking thinking tells you that another glass won't make any difference one way or the other. But those "just one more" thoughts and drinks add up. You drink three, four or more glasses of wine and you become inebriated. It's easy to get smashed when you engage in this kind of drinking thinking. Eliminate it - it's dangerous. One or two glasses of wine might not hurt, but more will.

"This is a such a special occasion, let's get drunk." The "alcohol makes a special occasion more special" excuse. Even if you're celebrating a truly joyous occasion - like getting accepted into college or getting married or graduating - do you really have to binge and get drunk to mark the occasion? You don't. If you get fried, you'll make yourself sick, you won't remember most of the party and you'll have a whopping hangover the next morning. And you'll associate this joyous occasion with a nasty hangover for the rest of your life. If you drink moderately, on the other hand, you'll feel great the next morning and have a lifetime of wonderful memories.

"I've been so good for such a long time, it's okay for me to get wasted." The "alcohol is my reward for not drinking" excuse. Rewarding yourself for not drinking by getting drunk? What kind of logic is that? It's not logical at all. Drinking because you haven't been drinking doesn't make sense. Another reason to cross off your drinking thinking list. You have too much integrity to justify your drinking with this lame excuse.

"Binge drinking is just a phase. I'll grow out of it, so I'm not going to stress about it right now." The "I'll worry about alcohol later" excuse. Handy when you're in a pinch and you really need to rationalize heavy drinking. In fact, many drinkers never outgrow binge drinking. They continue to binge for the rest of their lives. And you may or may not outgrow it. So stop thinking that bingeing is just a passing fancy. But you'll never have to worry about it if you don't binge in the first place! Payoff.

"My drinking is my own business and doesn't hurt anyone else." The "alcohol's my business" excuse. And it's not true. When you lose it, booze affects not only you, it affects everyone around you - your family, friends and strangers. You might clash with people you know or don't know and you might do dangerous things, like drinking and driving, that can hurt others. Drinking is not just your business and it's not a good reason to get drunk. However, if you drink smart, you'll never have to worry about negatively impacting your life or anyone else's because of liquor.

"I can handle my alcohol without any problems." The "I control alcohol" excuse. The truth is that after a couple of drinks, you are no longer in control, alcohol is. And the more you drink, the less control you have over your feelings, your actions and your reactions. So much for thinking that you're in charge when you've passed your drink limit. Liquor is and don't forget it. But if you drink smart and stick to your limit, you can control alcohol.

"Alcohol is not that harmful and there are lots of other things worse than booze. I don't do drugs." The "alcohol isn't that bad" excuse. Just because beer is legal doesn't mean it's harmless. Alcohol can be deadly - you can die from alcohol poisoning or kill or injure yourself and someone else when you're under the influence. Another excuse out the window. Liquor is a powerful drug and it should be used in moderation.

"I'm smarter than most people and can manage alcohol better than most people." The "I can outsmart alcohol" excuse. You think you're smarter than alcohol and tell yourself you don't abuse it, even if you binge and get drunk every once in a while. Newsflash: even the smartest people attending the best schools or working the best jobs can get into trouble with booze. Alcohol abuse has nothing to do with your IQ. Hopefully, you're smart enough to know this and you'll watch your alcohol consumption.

"I work hard and I play hard, so when I drink, I get wasted." The "it's okay to take alcohol to the extreme" excuse. You give one hundred percent to everything you do, so when you drink you give one hundred percent to beer too. Should you give food your all, gorge yourself and get fat? Should you give smoking your all and get lung cancer? Going overboard on anything is hazardous to your health. And you're not a wimp just because you don't get drunk when you drink. Scratch this excuse off your drinking thinking list right now.

"I have to have more drinks if my friends offer them to me. It's rude to refuse them." The "I'm rude if I refuse alcohol" excuse. How can you equate good manners with refusing drinks? You can't. It's silly to rationalize drinking by telling yourself you might offend someone if you turn down another drink. In fact, it's polite not to expose other people to a drunken you.

"I'd like to cut down or stop drinking, but I can't afford it." The "affordability of alcohol treatment" excuse. You're blaming your bad drinking habits on your pocketbook. This makes no sense because many moderate drinking and abstinence programs are free. No more excuses! You can afford to clean up. Nothing - not even money - can stop you if you really want to.

"I know when I've had enough, when to stop drinking and if it's safe to drive." The "I know my alcohol limit" excuse. The truth is you don't know your limit after a couple of drinks. More than that and the booze is talking - telling you you're sober enough and safe enough to do anything. Alcohol - even if it's only one or two drinks - and driving don't mix. Ever.

"I can stop drinking anytime I want to. And I don't want to right now." The "I don't have a problem with alcohol" excuse. You can prove you can stop drinking - by stopping. If it's too hard, then you know you have a drinking problem and you should do something about it. Either stop altogether or get with the smart drinking program. No more silly excuses or denial.

What will you say to yourself to defeat your drinking thinking? Control drinking thinking, control drinking.

Defeat Your Drinking Thinking

- *Become aware of thoughts, excuses and reasons that encourage your drinking*
- *Poke holes in the logic of those thoughts, reasons and excuses*
- *Replace those illogical thoughts, reasons and excuses with positive, logical ones that will support smart drinking*

Finally, Learn to Motivate Yourself to Stay On the Smart Drinking Track Forever

Motivation is the driving force behind your actions and it provides the energy and determination you need to follow through with smart drinking tips and guidelines, if you choose to drink. If you know how to motivate yourself, you can stay on the smart drinking track forever - your ultimate goal.

How do you fuel your motivation - so you get excited about controlling your drinking? You dream about all of the positive benefits that will be yours when you're a smart drinker. They're your payoffs or motivating factors.

For starters, think about how good you'll feel when you don't binge. You'll have tons of energy - you're no longer hung over or feeling slow from too much partying. And your increased energy will translate into increased activity and enthusiasm for life. You'll get a lot more done. Payoffs.

You'll also avoid serious alcohol-related health problems. Binge drinking can cause liver, pancreas, digestive, respiratory, kidney, heart disease and neurological problems. Drinking too much will probably shorten your lifespan. If you drink smart, however, you won't have to worry about these diseases and dying young from them. Payoff.

If you steer clear of problem drinking, you'll look better too. You'll be leaner and meaner. Alcohol is fattening, so if you drink heavily on a regular basis you're bound to gain weight. And you'll probably age more gracefully if you don't over drink. Liquor dehydrates you and causes premature wrinkles and aging. You'll avoid the sags and the bags, if you avoid bingeing. Feeling good, looking good, preventing serious alcohol-related illnesses and premature aging and death are all moderate drinking payoffs.

Your outlook on life will also be rosier - if you don't over do it. Remember - alcohol can actually cause or exacerbate emotional problems, stress, depression and anxiety. Sure, one or two drinks may relax you and improve your mood - short-term. That's smart drinking. But when you binge, get drunk, blackout and pass out, you feel awful the next day. You not only have a physical hangover, you have a psychological one as well. The emotional problems, stress, depression or anxiety come back worse than ever and you feel ashamed and embarrassed - deflating your self-esteem. A double whammy!

Say goodbye to self-esteem, self-confidence and a positive state of mind if you drink dumb. But say hello to stronger self-esteem, greater self-confidence and improved psychological health if you drink smart. More payoffs and powerful motivating factors to keep you on the moderate drinking track.

You'll have better relationships when you drink less. Liquor - when used in excess - destroys families and alienates friends. It makes you less inhibited, less reliable and less trustworthy. In contrast, the more you exercise control and moderation, the healthier your relationships with family, friends and colleagues will be. Booze won't get in the way, cause you to misbehave and keep people away. You'll also be a better parent and role model for your kids. The payoffs just keep on coming.

You'll be more productive at school or work too. No more hangovers to bog you down. You'll feel more like studying and attending class - translating into better grades at school. You'll have fewer sick days, be on top of your projects and be more likely to get a raise or promotion at work. You'll be better at what you do - if you drink smart. Another huge payoff.

Alcohol-related legal and financial problems would never cross your mind - if you control your drinking. All of the misery and expense caused by these problems simply wouldn't exist. You'd never worry about drinking and driving, because you'd never drink and drive. You'd never worry about an arrest record, because you'd never do anything stupid that could get you arrested. And you'd never have costly legal fees or financial problems caused by alcohol abuse. More big payoffs.

You'll also have more fun and enjoy life more - naturally - without so much beer. One of the dangers of drinking is thinking you can only have fun if you're high on booze. That's simply not true. You can actually have more fun if you're clean and sober or if you drink smart. You're not physically or psychologically impaired, so you can take in and appreciate the entire experience. And you're able to remember the good times - not like in the old days when you binged and blacked out. The payoffs keep coming.

Peace of mind is yours when you practice smart drinking. When you know you're not dependent on any substance for your good time, life is sweet. You can live your life to the fullest, because you're not worried about drinking or alcohol. What a relief. Another wonderful payoff.

What are your payoffs or motivating factors to drink smart? Record them and think of them often - everyday - and especially when you're facing a drinking party. Then, when you reach your drink limit, remind yourself of your payoffs. They'll give you the energy and determination you need to say no to another drink!

Payoffs or Motivating Factors to Stay On the Smart Drinking Track

- *You'll feel good*
- *You'll have more energy*
- *You'll be more productive*
- *You'll avoid alcohol-related health problems*
- *You'll live longer*
- *You'll look good*
- *You'll avoid obesity and premature aging*
- *You'll feel healthier psychologically*
- *You'll prevent or limit emotional or mood problems*
- *You'll enjoy greater self-esteem*
- *You'll enjoy greater self-confidence*
- *You'll have better relationships with family, friends and colleagues*
- *You'll be a better parent and role model*

- *You may get better grades in school*
- *You may get a raise or promotion at work*
- *You'll never worry about alcohol-related legal problems*
- *You'll never worry about alcohol-related financial problems*
- *You'll be sharper mentally and physically*
- *You'll lead a happier, more fulfilling life in general*
- *You'll never worry about being dependent on a substance*
- *You'll enjoy lasting peace of mind*

Teaser

How's your alcohol attitude adjustment coming? What are you doing to make booze less important in your life? What does your drinking thinking sound like? How are you countering it, so it doesn't encourage your drinking? Finally, make a list of all of the positive payoffs in store for you when you drink smart. Then think of them whenever you reach your drink limit and stop drinking!

Chapter Fifteen:
Live Well, Drink Less

A healthy, balanced lifestyle is the antidote to alcohol abuse. It's just easier to drink less when you feel good physically, feel good mentally and feel good about the world around you. Here are some simple tips for a healthier, happier you.

Eat Wisely

To drink smart, you need to eat smart. Why? Because a nutritious diet will decrease your desire to drink and binge. A sensible diet keeps you on an even keel - physically and mentally - so you have less interest in alcohol. When you eat wisely, you feel satisfied, your blood sugar levels remain stable, your mood remains stable and you're less likely to go off the deep end with booze. Great reasons to eat well!

Junk food, on the other hand, sets you up - physically and mentally - to drink and binge. Burgers, fries, nachos and sodas are convenient, but they slow you down, fatten you up and make you more susceptible to alcohol craving. When you eat junk, your blood sugar levels and mood yoyo which can increase your drinking desire and lead to problem drinking.

Start with lots of fresh fruits and vegetables. In fact, your diet should consist mainly of fruits and veggies. Get your fill of whole grains too. Throw in dairy products and eggs. And add fish or a little lean meat on the side and you have the makings of a smart diet.

Eat three light, well-balanced meals a day and have a couple of healthy snacks in between. Watch your portions - overeating even healthy foods won't produce the anti-alcohol craving effect you're looking for. And pre-plan your daily menu, much like you pre-plan your drinking, so you can avoid impulsive food decisions.

In the morning have fruit, whole grain cereal and milk or yogurt. Mid-morning, make room for a high-fiber nutrition or energy bar light on fat and calories. For lunch, how about a salad or bowl of soup? Have a hearty snack around three or four in the afternoon - apples and peanut butter or cheese and whole wheat crackers? And a light dinner of fish or chicken plus a veggie should round out your day.

Keep fatty, high-calorie, processed fast foods to a minimum. You can still frequent your favorite fast food joints every once in a while. Just try to stick to the healthier choices on the menu. And if you can't resist that taco or burger, try to limit it to once a week, instead of every other day.

Eating healthy is not rocket science. Stick with it for just one week and see how good you feel. Most importantly, observe how your sensible eating habits stabilize your mood and decrease your desire to drink.

Work It

Blowing off steam with exercise will also weaken your need to drink and binge - in addition to alleviating stress, depression and anxiety. All you have to do is get up off your bottom four or five times a week - every day if possible - and get moving.

Get busy with a workout you enjoy. What activities have you liked in the past? What activities have you always dreamed of doing, but have never gotten around to? Tennis, running, soccer, baseball, basketball, football, skiing, pumping iron, bicycling, rowing, swimming, hiking, mountain biking, surfing, workout CDs, yoga, dancing? If they worked for you in the past, they might be just as much fun for you now. And if you've always wanted to try something new, this is your golden opportunity to go for it.

Exercise doesn't have to kill you and it doesn't have to be limited to a sport. It can be gardening, tai chi, vacuuming, walking the dog, taking the stairs, instead of the elevator and parking your car a mile from the grocery store so you take in a stroll. Just pump up your everyday physical activity and you won't have to go out of your way to get fit.

Mix it up, have some fun and get your heart pumping for at least thirty minutes four or five times a week and you'll reap the benefits - a better body, a better attitude, less alcohol craving and smarter drinking. Do it!

What's on your exercise agenda for today? What's on your exercise agenda for this week? Make plans right now. At the end of the week, ask yourself if you feel less stressed and have a greater sense of well-being. Also ask yourself if regular exercise steps on your desire to drink.

Catch Your Z's

Seventy percent of all Americans are sleep deprived. Are you one of them? If you are, you not only feel tired most of the time, you probably feel edgy and have a bad attitude too. You may also have a hard time concentrating, you're more impulsive and you're unable to make sound decisions - including sound drinking decisions. If, however, you got at least seven hours of sound sleep every night, you'd have plenty of energy, a better attitude, you'd be able to concentrate and you'd be capable of making wiser decisions - including wiser drinking decisions.

Sleeping in is not as difficult as you may think. Simply pre-plan how long you want to rest and give yourself plenty of time to achieve your goal. Try getting to bed an hour earlier or staying in bed an hour later, if possible, to get the sleep you need. Avoid caffeine and eating too late - they'll keep you up. And avoid doing things that require serious thinking just before you turn in - like playing sudoku or doing homework. You'll have a harder time settling down and falling asleep because your brain is still on when the lights go off.

Make your bedroom into a peaceful oasis conducive to sleep too. Turn off all electronic and communication devices. That includes cell phones, pagers, TVs, laptops, PCs, iphones, texting devices, blackberries and ipods. You don't want anything to stimulate you and prevent you from getting lots of wonderful sleep. Get plenty of fresh air, pull the curtains so you're not disturbed by light, have cuddly warm blankets on hand, add a couple of calming green plants and your bedroom oasis will be complete. Embrace the comfort and quiet and sleep. Sweet dreams!

What's your plan to catch up on your sleep? How does sleeping - or not sleeping - affect your mood and your drinking?

Have Some Good, Clean Fun

Good, clean fun. Not clear on the concept? We're all so busy these days we've forgotten what it is or how to have it. We rely on alcohol for instant entertainment instead. But when you rediscover alcohol-free fun, you'll rediscover you can have a great time without booze. A must for smart drinking success.

If you haven't a clue on how to have alcohol-free fun, first look to your past. What did you do for kicks in the good old days? Camping, going to the movies, laying by the pool, hiking, eating popcorn, watching CDs, traveling, going to concerts, cooking, playing tennis, flirting, writing your novel, painting a picture, fly fishing, playing monopoly, snorkeling, playing chess, having a dinner party, taking pictures, exploring caves, making ice cream, having a cookout on the beach, having a sleepover, going to a football or baseball game? Remember what use to turn you on and give it another try.

Now think of things you've always wanted to do, but have never gotten around to. Learning to ski or play golf? Going to Yosemite or Hawaii? Having a picnic in the woods? Learning to dance? Learning to surf? Going on a hayride? Building sand castles? Taking up horseback riding? Checking out a car show? Going to the county fair? Soaking in a mineral bath and having a massage? Learning how to make jewelry? Going to a cooking school? Becoming a Big Brother or Big Sister? Learning how to play an instrument? Joining a softball team? Starting a band? Baking bread? Joining a book club? Brainstorm all the fun things you'd like to do. Then do them.

Interesting people and activities - that don't involve liquor - open up a whole new world to you. A healthier world where you don't have to drink to enjoy yourself. And just that thought makes you less dependent on alcohol.

What good, clean fun - minus beer - do you have planned for this week? What good, clean fun do you have planned for the next month? Plan at least two entertaining alcohol-free activities each week and go for it. What have you got to lose? A drinking problem!

Does having fun - without alcohol - help you put liquor in perspective? It should. Do you drink less because of it? You should.

Enjoy Healthy Relationships

Getting along with your family and keeping company with positive people is another aspect of a balanced, healthy lifestyle. And the happier and more fulfilling your relationships are, the easier it will be for you to turn down alcohol.

What makes for healthy family relations? Try to communicate openly for starters. Being able to talk to your parents or guardians about important issues, like school, peer pressure, dating and the physiological and emotional changes you're going through, would be great. But if honest communication about hot topics is not possible, suggest getting a third party involved to open up the lines of communication and improve family relationships. A trusted friend, your clergyman or a mental health professional may be able to help.

Other things you can do to nurture family relations? How about being objective, looking at all your parents do for you, appreciating their efforts and telling them you're grateful for the sacrifices they make for you. A simple "thank you" a couple of times a week would go a long way to make things better.

Making an effort to connect with your brothers and sisters would also improve your family life. How about spending some time with them and communicating with them respectfully, instead of brushing them off. Making an effort to get involved in family matters and events would help too. Participate in family game and movie nights. And go on the family vacation and join in the fun - instead of avoiding it all costs.

Your parents and siblings love you, even though you may not think so at times. Take notice when they do something nice for you and thank them for it. Appreciating the family, actively participating in family gatherings and being polite and respectful to all of the members of your family might just transform your unhappy family life into a happy one. You might just like your family, if you gave them a chance and got to know them!

What qualities make for healthy, satisfying relationships in general - whether they're family, friends or romantic relationships? Trust. Knowing you can open up to someone who has your best interests at heart and will keep your conversation confidential is a must. Respect. One definition of respect is to honor. For a friend to sincerely honor you in a relationship is also another must. Honesty. A person being straight with you about everything - or almost everything - is also essential to cultivate a meaningful relationship. There is no room in a healthy relationship for dishonesty.

Equality. Treating each other as equals is also required to make good friends. If either one of you think you're better than the other, there's no respect and no real friendship. Boundaries. Knowing your limits and your friend's limits is another important quality of a mutual friendship. If you or your pal ask too much of each other, you put your relationship in jeopardy. If you trust and respect each other, treat each other as equals and are honest with each other, you won't overstep your boundaries and you'll remain friends.

And what qualities make for unhealthy or abusive relationships - whether they're family, friends or romantic relationships? No communication or abusive communication. Being untrustworthy. Being disrespectful. Being dishonest. Not being treated as an equal. Overstepping boundaries. Not taking responsibility for one's behavior in the relationship. Being physically, emotionally or verbally abusive. Being isolated in the relationship. Being controlled in the relationship. These are all red flags that indicate an unhealthy relationship.

And finally, how can you connect with others of like mind and cultivate wholesome new relationships? How about looking into organized activities where you can meet other people who have the same interests you have. The tennis club, if you're a tennis player. The jazz band, if you love to jam. Join the Sierra Club, if you dig the outdoors. Take a yoga class and make friends with others into mind/body practices. Get involved in the drama club, if you like to act.

Keep an mind open and you can start up a friendship with anyone, anywhere, anytime - an interesting person in one of your classes, at work, at the coffee shop or through another friend. You're probably bumping into people all day long you have a lot in common with. Open your eyes, be friendly and you'll make more friends without even trying.

There you have it. How to cultivate happier, healthier relation-ships with family, friends and lovers in a nutshell. What relationships of yours need tending? How will you improve them? What's your plan to get out, circulate and make new friends? Do it! Having good people around you feels so much better than getting high on booze.

Nurture Strong Self-Esteem

What is self-esteem? It's what you think of yourself. And the more pleased you are with yourself, the less interest you'll have in mind-altering substances. When you like yourself, who needs beer to feel better? Not you!

How can you pump up your self-esteem - short of professional help? The first thing you should do is to focus on your strengths. Everybody's good at something, that goes for you too. Are you smarter than most people, more athletic than most people, funnier than most people, more organized than most people, more musical than most people, a better friend than most people, have a great personality? Can you do magic tricks or make a great pizza? What are you good at? Make a list of your assets and never forget them.

Second, be realistic and accepting of yourself. You're not perfect, nobody is. If you're not a good basketball player or you have a big nose, accept it and move on. You can't really do much about it. Just like you have a list of impressive talents, you also have some shortcomings. Again, focus on your strong points, not your weak ones.

Third, set reasonable goals for yourself. Not everyone is cut out to go to Harvard. How about applying to the local community college where you're sure to get in and make the dean's list. Or forget about a career in musical theatre, if you can't carry a tune. Find another job in the entertainment field and stick to singing in the shower instead. Or ditch the idea of becoming a doctor, if you can't stand the sight of blood. Consider another healthcare profession that doesn't require surgery. The more realistic you are in setting your goals, the more likely you'll achieve them and excel. And the better you'll feel about yourself.

Fourth, be patient when working towards your lofty goals. Want to earn a college degree, but can't imagine going to school full-time for four or five years? Take it easy, don't get ahead of yourself and concentrate on just one semester at a time until you have your diploma in hand. Want to make tons of money? You'll probably have to work your way up through the ranks before you earn the big bucks. Think of achieving your goals as climbing a ladder. Each step gets you a little closer to the prize. And remind yourself that most big goals don't happen overnight. They're accomplished by taking lots of little baby steps over time - until you make the grade. Something to think about when you're shooting for the moon.

Fifth, give yourself a pat on the back for all of your small victories. Maybe you aced the science final or you were chosen to play a solo in the band or you got your driver's license or you got a raise at work. Give yourself credit where credit is due. It's called positive rein-forcement - a wonderful way to strengthen your self-esteem and self-confidence and prepare you for even bigger challenges ahead.

Sixth, stop telling yourself you're a loser! Putting yourself down and telling yourself you're not smart enough, not good looking enough, not thin enough, not popular enough, not athletic enough or not talented enough serves no good purpose, except to make you feel bad about yourself. If you do fall short at times, don't beat yourself up. Get up, get on with your life and put your best foot forward.

The next time you catch yourself talking trash to yourself, replace those negative thoughts with positive ones - thoughts of your assets and accomplishments. Obsessing about what's wrong with you is counterproductive. And it won't take you where you want to go in life.

Seventh, acknowledge the nice things you do everyday. Maybe it's helping a friend, giving a compliment, making a fabulous dinner or being kind to a person in need. Celebrate yourself! Your self-esteem and self-confidence will grow and flourish when you realize what a nice person you are.

Eighth, surround yourself with supportive people. Good friends encourage you to better yourself and are there for you in a pinch. They provide that little push you need at times to be the best you can be. Good friends are self-esteem and self-confidence boosters. Dump anyone you can't trust and anyone who is physically, emotionally or verbally abusive to you. They drag you and your self-esteem down. You deserve better than that!

Ninth, get out and do things that will make you feel good about yourself. Bake cookies for your grandma, volunteer at the soup kitchen, clean the house for a sick neighbor, cleanup the creek, build houses for Habitat for Humanity, support schools in Central America, teach your little brother or sister how to swim. When you make an effort to do nice things for other people, it makes you feel good about yourself. And that's what strong self-esteem is all about.

Tenth, respect yourself and treat yourself well. Take care of yourself - physically and psychologically. You're worth it. If you treat yourself carelessly, you're sending the wrong message to yourself - that you're not wonderful and you don't deserve to be handled with care. Treat yourself like your very best friend and you'll never worry about low self-esteem again!

If these ten tips to increase your self-esteem don't do the trick, be assertive and talk to a trusted friend, parent, counselor or psychologist about getting on the strong self-esteem track. It's that important.

What brings you and your self-esteem up? What are the assets and accomplishments you're most proud of? List them. What brings you and your self-esteem down? Grades, relationships, looks? List them. Then do something about them or accept them and move on. Whatever makes you feel best. The stronger your self-esteem is, the weaker your need for alcohol will be.

Get Your Priorities Straight

Setting priorities is another way to improve and balance your life. Prioritizing means you tend to your most important projects and goals first and save the other less important ones for later. If you prioritize, you'll reduce both your stress level and your desire to drink.

If you're like most young people, you lead a hectic life. You're constantly juggling school, work, a social life, a love life, family and money pressures. And you're bombarded with electronic devices. Sometimes, you don't know if you're coming or you're going.

When you feel overwhelmed because you have too much to do, it may be difficult to know where to start. That's where prioritizing comes in. Start with your most important tasks first, like taking care of yourself and being prepared for school and work. Make sure you eat healthy, exercise and have clean clothes for the day ahead. Make sure you've studied and you're prepared for class. Or make sure you get to work on time. You'll take the pressure off and sleep well at night when you tackle the big stuff first.

Less important tasks can wait. Like watching movies. Or practicing with the band. Or hanging out and socializing. Or playing softball. Or going to the beach. Or playing poker. Yes, fun is important, but fit it in when you can - after more urgent matters have been taken care of.

What are your priorities? Decide in advance what you need to get done for the day, for the week, for the month and for the year. Prioritizing will defuse your stress and your drinking.

Put Your Life in Perspective

Putting your life in perspective will balance it and dampen your desire to drink. When you take the long view of things, you realize what's really important to you. You're less confused and more focused. And alcohol is no longer an issue for you.

How do you put your life in perspective? First, you've got to look at the big picture. What are the most important things to you in your life? Robust health, good grades, going to college, falling in love, professional achievement, traveling, loyal friends, getting married, making millions, becoming a parent, cleaning up the planet, a loving family? What are the least important? Beer, doing laundry, learning to cook, cleaning the apartment, vodka? When you decide what's really important to you, you'll have a different point of view of yourself and your life.

Second, adopt a "nothing is the end of the world" attitude. Not being blown off by the person you're into. Not making the team. Not making the dean's list. Not getting into the college you want to get into. Not going to Europe for the summer. Not having the money to go shopping. Not making a high SAT score. Not getting the job you want. Nothing is the end of the world. You will survive and thrive - no matter what happens. That should be your first thought when facing tough challenges and putting your life in perspective.

Third, when things aren't going well, stop, take a step back and gather your senses. Yes, it's normal to feel disappointed and unhappy when you get bad news. That's when you need to take a deep breath, calm down and feel confident you'll make it through the crisis. You'll pick yourself up, dust yourself off and endure the initial shock. And you'll feel better in no time. Remember that the next time you hit a bump in the road.

Fourth, appreciate what you already have. What good qualities, talents, resources, skills and successes have helped you so far? Are you smart, athletic, witty, compassionate, thoughtful, creative, musical, analytical, expressive, loving? Be grateful for what you've got and everything else will fall into place.

Finally, when life gets you down and you feel like you're losing perspective, be patient. There may not be instant solutions to all of the problems you'll encounter in life. Maybe some answers will come to you over time. And if a problem's not solvable, you'll have to learn to live with it. Hang tight, take your time and don't do anything rash that you'll regret later. Remember - time is on your side and things are bound to get better.

What can you do to put your life in perspective? Be more objective about your life and you'll be more objective about alcohol.

Cultivate a Spiritual Practice

Cultivating a spiritual practice is another means to help you achieve a healthier, more balanced lifestyle. What are the benefits of a spiritual practice? Peace of mind. Feeling calmer. Feeling more secure. Feeling more connected to other people. Feeling more connected to the world. Feeling a power greater than yourself is in charge. Feeling that regardless of life's ups and downs, you can always rely on something bigger and better to see you through. Feeling you no longer need alcohol to soothe your soul.

A spiritual practice might enable you to see every person as a friend, not an enemy - because we're all expressions of a greater being. It might motivate you to do better by yourself and others - you'd be more inclined to spread the love around. And it might make you feel more satisfied in general.

Believing in and acting on positive spiritual beliefs might make you physically and psychologically healthier. It might lower your blood pressure and relieve other health problems. It might reduce or eliminate stress, depression or anxiety. And it might increase your overall happiness. Spiritual practice is an all-natural stress reducer and mood enhancer!

If you're not into it already, it would be worth your while to explore different spiritual paths and see which one works for you. Improve the quality of your life that is. Traditional, organized religion? Eastern philosophies - Buddhism, Hinduism or yoga? New age or nature-based approaches? Find one that clicks with you, surrender yourself to something bigger than you are and enjoy.

Thoughtful spiritual practice might fill the void in your life that you've been filling with booze. Think about it.

Live Well, Drink Less Lifestyle Tips

- *Eat wisely*
- *Work it*
- *Catch your Z's*
- *Have some good, clean fun*
- *Enjoy healthy relationships*
- *Nurture strong self-esteem*
- *Get your priorities straight*
- *Put your life in perspective*
- *Cultivate a spiritual practice*

Teaser

What lifestyle changes might curb your alcohol appetite? A better diet, more exercise, more rest, good, clean fun, healthier relationships, stronger self-esteem, setting your priorities, putting your life in perspective, cultivating a spiritual practice? Get with the healthy lifestyle program and eliminate your need to drink.

Part V:
Get Support

Chapter Sixteen: Is This Smart Drinking Guide Enough?

You don't have to live with a drinking problem. If moderate drinking doesn't work for you, it's up to you to look into different abstinence approaches that will.

Here are more options to address your drinking. Plus tips on how to choose a college with an effective drinking prevention program.

Look Into Individual Counseling

You might consider counseling with a licensed mental health professional who specializes in young people with substance abuse problems. Maybe they can help you with your specific situation and point you in the right direction.

Look Into Family Counseling

If family relationships and dynamics are driving you to drink, perhaps you should look into sorting out your problems at home with a licensed mental health professional who specializes in family relationships and alcohol abuse. Maybe they can help you and your parents resolve the issues coming between you, so you don't cope with alcohol.

Give SADD a Try

Students Against Drunk Driving (SADD) may be able to give you the tips and support you need to stay on the sobriety track. Check out their website at: www.sadd.org.

Give AA a Try

Or Alcoholics Anonymous may be the way to go. Some people swear by it and the Twelve Step program. Attend an open meeting or two and see if it could work for you. Check out their website at: www.alcoholics-anonymous.org

Check Out NCADI Live Help

The National Clearinghouse for Alcohol and Drug Information is staffed by trained information specialists who can answer your questions about drinking and alcohol 24 hours a day.

Call Toll-Free : 1-800-729-6686
Se habla espanol: 1-877-767-8432
Washington, D.C. 301-468-2600
TDD: 1-800-487-4889
Fax: 301-468-6433
For a confidential online text chat with an NCADI information specialist, logon to: www.health.org/help/default.aspx.

Check Out the National Drug and Alcohol Treatment Referral Routing Service

Call them to speak to someone about an alcohol problem and for more information about treatment programs in your local community.

Call Toll-Free : 1-800-662-HELP
Or logon to this link for frequently asked questions:
www.niaaa.nih.gov/faq/faq.htm.

Tips For Evaluating Alcohol Abuse Prevention Programs At Colleges

If you attend a college with an effective drinking prevention program that does not condone alcohol use or binge drinking, you will reduce your exposure to drinking situations and your risk of developing a serious drinking problem.

Here are some questions you should ask to determine a school's alcohol policies and attitudes and if it's a party school where lots of drinking and bingeing takes place.

— Do you have campus alcohol policies? What are they?
— Do you have a drinking prevention program, counseling and follow-up services for students who abuse alcohol? If they don't have a drinking prevention program or counseling services available for drinkers, you should think twice about attending.
— Do you have alcohol-free dorms? If they do, that's good and it means you have an alcohol-free living option.
— Does campus housing have residential advisors or dorm monitors? If they do, that's good and it means you'll have someone watching out for you and discouraging rowdy drinking parties.

— How much influence do fraternities and sororities have on campus? The more influence fraternities and sororities have, the more likely it's a party school.
— What percentage of classes are held on Fridays? The more the better. Students don't get a head start on weekend drinking if classes are held on Friday.
— What's the average number of years it takes to graduate from the school? If it takes too long, it's probably a party school.
— How many liquor law violations and alcohol-related injuries or deaths have occurred in recent years at the school? If there are a lot, this school isn't for you.
— Check out the school newspaper for ads for parties, bars and security incidents. Again, if there are lots of party and bar listings and campus arrests, this school isn't for you.

If the school has a lax attitude about liquor, no policies about alcohol use and no drinking prevention program on campus, you might want to rethink going there. Drinking and bingeing may be part of the curriculum. Not your kind of school.

Chapter Seventeen:
Resources for Young Drinkers, Parents, Educators and Communities

A Matter of Degree (AMOD)

www.amodstrat.net

An advocacy group administered by the American Medical Association dedicated to reducing alcohol abuse among college students and improving the quality of life in the community.

Al-Anon/Alateen

www.al-anon.alateen.org

A worldwide organization for people concerned about someone else's drinking.

Alcohol 101

www.alcohol101plus.org

Explores decisions in at-risk college settings.

Alcohol Screening.org

Assess your drinking, get information about alcohol and health and review links to resources, including a database of twelve thousand treatment centers.

Alcoholics Anonymous

www.alcoholics-anonymous.org
A worldwide recovery program with meetings in most communities.

BACCHUS

www.bacchusgamma.org
A college and university based peer network focusing on student, young adult, campus and communitywide leadership on health and safety issues.

Be Responsible About Drinking (BRAD)

www.brad21.org
Offers educational information about alcohol and was founded by the family and friends of Bradley McCue - a college student who died of alcohol poisoning after celebrating his twenty-first birthday.

Break Away

www.alternativebreaks.org
An organization promoting alcohol-free spring breaks.

Center for Alcohol Marketing and Youth (CAMY)

www.camy.org
Offers fact sheets, alcohol marketing information and research on alcohol and youth.

Center for Substance Abuse Prevention

www.samhsa.gov/centers/csap/csap.html
A federal program to prevent alcohol, tobacco and illegal drug problems.

CIRCLe Network
www.circlenetwork.org
A non-profit organization dedicated to improving the quality of life on campus.

The CORE Institute
www.coreinstitute.com
Funded by the federal government, its mission is to assist colleges and universities in alcohol and drug prevention efforts.

Daily Dose
www.dailydose.net
Contains articles about substance misuse and abuse from the World Wide Web.

Drink/Link Moderate Drinking Programs and Products
www.drinklinkmoderation.com
Offers moderate drinking programs teaching sensible alcohol use to prevent alcoholism.

Facts on Tap
www.fastsontap.org
Offers alcohol prevention initiatives targeting teen and college students.

The Gordie Foundation
www.thegordiefoundation.org
Dedicated to the memory of Gordie Bailey, a University of Colorado college student who died of alcohol poisoning during a fraternity initiation in 2004, its mission is to provide young people with the skills to avoid the dangers of alcohol through education and promotion of self-worth.

Hazelden

www.hazelden.org

Offers adolescent and young adult chemical assessment and treatment.

Higher Education Center for Alcohol and Other Drug Information (HEC)

www.edc.org/hec

HEC's mission is to reduce student problems related to alcohol, drugs and interpersonal violence by helping colleges to develop, implement and evaluate programs and policies.

Join Together

www.jointogether.org

Offers a news service, hosts online discussion groups and lists resources and funding sources for people and groups working to prevent substance abuse.

Leadership to Keep Children Alcohol Free

www.alcoholfreechildren.org.

Federal, public and private organizations come together to prevent alcohol use by children ages nine to fifteen.

The Marin Institute for the Prevention of Alcohol and Other Drug Problems

www.marininstitute.org

Focuses on environments that encourage and glamorize alcohol use. It also offers a database of alcohol policy resources and information about the alcohol beverage industry.

Mothers Against Drunk Driving (MADD)

www.madd.org

Offers counseling for victims and information on activities.

National Alliance to Prevent Underage Drinking

www.cspinet.org

A coalition of public health, education, consumer, law enforcement, religious, child and family welfare, substance abuse treatment and prevention and other national organizations dedicated to building and sustaining a broad societal commitment to reduce underage drinking.

National Association for Addiction Professionals

www.naadac.org

Its mission is to lead, unify and empower addiction focused professionals to achieve excellence through education, advocacy, knowledge, standards of practice, ethics, product development and research.

National Center on Addiction and Substance Abuse at Columbia University (CASA)

www.casacolumbia.org

A think tank that studies substance abuse and its effects on society.

National Clearinghouse for Alcohol and Drug Information (NCADI) Live Help

www.health.org

A federal government organization which claims to be the world's largest resource for information on substance abuse. It also has a staff of trained information specialists who can answer your questions 24 hours a day.

Call Toll-Free : 1-800-729-6686

Se habla espanol: 1-877-767-8432

Washington, D.C. 301-468-2600

TDD: 1-800-487-4889

Fax: 301-468-6433

For a confidential online text chat with an NCADI information specialist, logon to: www.health.org/help/default.aspx.

National Commission Against Drunk Driving (NCADD)

www.ncadd.com

Its mission is to reduce impaired driving by uniting public and private sector organizations and individuals.

National Crime Prevention Council

www.ncpc.org

An educational organization dedicated to helping individuals, neighborhoods, communities and governments prevent crime.

National Drug and Alcohol Treatment Referral Routing Service

www.niaaa.nih.gov/faq/faq.htm.

Offered by the Center for Substance Abuse Treatment, you can speak to someone about an alcohol problem and for more information about treatment programs in your local community.

Call Toll-Free : 1-800-662-HELP

Or logon to this link for frequently asked questions: www.niaaa.nih.gov/faq/faq.htm.

National Institute on Alcohol Abuse and Alcoholism

www.collegedrinkingprevention.gov

Provides high school students, college students and parents with information about bingeing.

National Institute on Alcohol Abuse and Alcoholism Substance Abuse Treatment Facility Locator

www.findtreatment.samhsa.gov

A guide to alcohol abuse treatment facilities in the United States.

National Substance Abuse Web Index

http://nsawi.health.org

Offers information on and links to substance abuse prevention and treatment communities.

Office of National Drug Control Policy (ONDCP)

www.whitehousedrugpolicy.gov

Sets policies and objectives for the United States Drug Control Program to reduce illicit drug use, manufacturing and trafficking and drug-related health problems, crime and violence.

Outside the Classroom

www.outsidetheclassroom.com

Offers cost-effective products to prevent alcohol abuse on campus.

Pacific Institute for Research and Evaluation (PIRE)

www.pire.org

Dedicated to promoting and evaluating activities, studies and programs that improve individual and public health, welfare and safety.

STOP Underage Drinking

www.stopalcoholabuse.gov

Information on underage drinking and strategies to combat it for parents, educators, community-based organizations and young people.

Students Against Destructive Decisions (SADD)

www.saddonline.com

Offers information on international prevention programs for junior and senior high school and college students to help them deal with underage drinking, drunk driving and drug abuse issues.

Substance Abuse and Mental Health Services Administration

www.ncadi.samhsa.gov

Offers information about alcohol abuse and alcoholism.

Task Force on College Drinking

www.collegedrinkingprevention.gov
Sponsored by the National Institute on Alcohol Abuse and Alcoholism (NIAAA), the task force focuses on alcohol abuse on college campuses and possible solutions to it.

The Trauma Foundation

www.tf.org/tf/alcohol
Its mission is to prevent alcohol-related injuries and deaths among young people.

Part VI:
For More Information . . .

About the Author

Donna J. Cornett, M.A.

Donna J. Cornett is the founder and director of Drink/Link Moderate Drinking Programs and Products. She holds a Master's Degree and California College Teaching Credential in psychology and believes offering drinkers a moderate drinking goal, instead of life-long abstinence, is the key to motivating them to seek early treatment and to preventing alcoholism.

Cornett was in her thirties when she realized she was drinking too much and would be facing a serious drinking problem if she did not address it. At that time, her only options were abstinence, AA or to keep drinking. There was no middle-of-the-road alcohol education program teaching drinkers sensible drinking habits and attitudes so they could avoid alcohol abuse. But like many drinkers, she did not believe her drinking was serious enough stop altogether or in the concept of a higher power to help her cut down.

Consequently, Cornett developed Drink/Link in 1988 - long before any other moderate drinking programs were available in the United States. This commonsense program teaches drinkers to modify their drinking habits, reduce alcohol craving and consumption and prevent alcoholism.

Donna J. Cornett is also the author of *7 Weeks to Safe Social Drinking: How to Effectively Moderate Your Alcohol Intake, Moderate Drinking - Naturally! Herbs and Vitamins to Control Your Drinking* and *The Moderate Drinking Made Easy Workbook: Drinker-Friendly Tips and Exercises to Control Drinking and Reduce Alcohol Craving and Consumption.* She has been featured or consulted for articles in Time Magazine, the New York Post, ABCNews.com, WebMD.com, Esquire, Scripps Howard News Service and professional publications. Her latest achievement is offering drinkers everywhere the first affordable, over-the-counter alcohol abuse prevention program - The Sensible Drinking System.

To contact Donna Cornett, email her at:
info@drinklinkmoderation.com,
call her at 707-539-5465
or write her at P.O. Box 5441, Santa Rosa, California 95402, USA.

About Drink/Link ™ Moderate Drinking Programs and Products

Drink/Link Moderate Drinking Programs and Products was established in 1988 and has helped thousands of drinkers worldwide to modify their drinking habits and attitudes, reduce their alcohol craving and consumption and prevent alcoholism. Drink/Link was the first moderate drinking program in the United States and the first one registered with both the California Department of Drug and Alcohol Programs and the United States Department of Health and Human Services.

All Drink/Link Programs are based on commonsense safe drinking guidelines and clinically-proven behavioral, cognitive, motivational and lifestyle strategies and techniques to stay within those guidelines. The most intensive programs, which include professional counseling, are the Email Counseling Program and the Telephone Counseling Program. The Self-Study Program and the Sensible Drinking System are self-help programs you complete on your own at home.

Drink/Link also offers a line of moderate drinking products. Contact Drink/Link directly at www.drinklinkmoderation.com to view the product catalog.

Drink/Link ™
Moderate Drinking Programs and Products
P.O. Box 5441
Santa Rosa, California USA 95402
Email: info@drinklinkmoderation.com
www.drinklinkmoderation.com
Local: 707-539-5465
Toll-Free: 888-773-7465
Fax: 707-537-1010

Drink/Link ™
Moderate Drinking Programs
and Products Order Forms

Order Your Own Copies of

7 Weeks to Safe Social Drinking:
How to Effectively Moderate Your Alcohol Intake
By Donna J. Cornett

Moderate Drinking - Naturally!
Herbs and Vitamins to Control Your Drinking
By Donna J. Cornett

The Moderate Drinking Made Easy Workbook
Drinker-Friendly Tips and Exercises to Control Drinking
and Reduce Your Alcohol Craving and Consumption
By Donna J. Cornett

PLEASE CIRCLE BOOKS OF CHOICE

7 Weeks to Safe Social Drinking	$18.95
Moderate Drinking - Naturally!	$18.95

Number of books:	Cost of books:
Shipping & Handling: (U.S. $4.95 for the first book. Outside U.S. $6.95 for the first and $4.95 for each additional book. Shipped U.S. Mail.)	
Subtotal:	
State Tax: (California residents please add tax)	
Final Total:	
Payment Enclosed	Please charge to my credit card (Visa, MasterCard, American Express)

Account #

Expiration Date:

Signature:

PLEASE SEND TO:

Name:

Institution:

Address:

City:	State/Zip:
Country:	Telephone:

Email:

Drink/Link™
Moderate Drinking Programs and Products
P.O. Box 5441
Santa Rosa, California USA 95402
Local: 707-539-5465 Toll-Free: 888-773-7465
Fax: 707-537-1010
Email: info@drinklinkmoderation.com
www.drinklinkmoderation.com

Drink/Link™
Moderate Drinking Programs and Products

ORDER FORM

**FOR A COMPLETE LISTING OF PROGRAMS AND PRODUCTS
LOGON TO:**
www.drinklinkmoderation.com
Local: 707- 539-5465
Toll-Free: 888-773-7465

The Drink/Link Self-Study Program - $195.00

This program includes a 50-minute telephone consultation with Donna Cornett personally - examining your current drinking habits and offering you tips to drink less tailored to your lifestyle. Also included is the workbook, *7 Weeks to Safe Social Drinking*, the CD, "Control Your Drinking - Now!", a Drinking Diary, Drink Graph, Nutritional Supplements and Step-by-Step Instructions so you can successfully complete the program on your own at home.

The Sensible Drinking System - $65.00

This over-the-counter program offers the basics - the workbook, *7 Weeks to Safe Social Drinking*, the CD, "Control Your Drinking - Now!", a Drinking Diary, Drink Graph and Step-by-Step Instructions so you can successfully complete the program on your own at home.

PLEASE CIRCLE THE PROGRAM OF CHOICE

The Drink/Link Self-Study Program $195.00

The Drink/Link Sensible Drinking System $65.00

Number of programs:	Cost of programs:
Shipping & Handling: (U.S. $10.00 for the first program. Outside U.S. $15.00 for the first and $10.00 for each additional program. Shipped U.S. Mail.)	
Subtotal:	
State Tax: (California residents please add tax)	
Final Total:	
Payment Enclosed	**Please charge to my credit card** (Visa, MasterCard, American Express)

Account #

Expiration Date:

Signature:

PLEASE SEND TO:

Name:

Institution:

Address:

City:	State/Zip:
Country:	Telephone:

Email:

Drink/Link™
Moderate Drinking Programs and Products
P.O. Box 5441
Santa Rosa, California USA 95402
Local: 707-539-5465 Toll-Free: 888-773-7465
Fax: 707-537-1010
Email: info@drinklinkmoderation.com
www.drinklinkmoderation.com

Bibliography

Bourne, Edmund. *The Anxiety and Phobia Workbook, Third Edition.* Oakland, California: New Harbinger Publications, 2002.

Centers for Disease Control and Prevention. "Alcohol-Related Disease Impact" available at www.cdc.gov/alcohol/ardi.htm.

Centers for Disease Control and Prevention. "Frequently Asked Questions - Alcohol" available at www.cdc.gov/alcohol/faqs.htm.

Columbia University National Center on Addiction and Substance Abuse (CASA). *2002 National Survey of American Attitudes on Substance Abuse VII: Teens, Parents and Siblings* available at www.casacolumbia.org.

Cornett, Donna. *7 Weeks to Safe Social Drinking: How to Effectively Moderate Your Alcohol Intake.* Santa Rosa, California: People Friendly Books, 2005.

Fox, Annie and Kirschner, Ruth. *Too Stressed To Think? A Teen Guide to Staying Sane When Life Makes You Crazy.* Minneapolis MN: Free Spirit Publishing, 2005.

Harper, Nancy L., Alcohol Laboratories for Education, Research and Training. "21 Reasons for Teens to Avoid Alcohol." Grand Valley State University, August 2005.

Harper, Nancy L., Alcohol Laboratories for Education, Research and Training. "What You Can Do to Stay Safe At a Party." Grand Valley State University, August 2004.

Harvard School of Public Health. 1993-2001 College Alcohol Study (CAS) available at www.hsph.harvard.edu/cas.

Heather, Nick and Robertson, Ian. *Controlled Drinking.* London: Plenum Press, 1983.

Hingson R.W., Heeren T., Jamanka A. and Howland, J. "Age of onset and unintentional injury involvement after drinking." *Journal of the American Medical Association* 2000; 284(12).

Hingson, R., Heeren, T. and Winter, M. "Lower legal blood alcohol limits for young drinkers." *Public Health Reports* 1994; 109.

Hingson, R.W., Heeren, T., Winter, M. and Wechsler, H. "Magnitude of alcohol-related mortality and morbidity among U.S. college students ages 18-24: Changes from 1998 to 2001." *Annual Review of Public Health* 2005; 26.

Howard, George S. and Nathan, Peter E. *Alcohol Use and Misuse By Young Adults.* Notre Dame, Indiana: University of Notre Dame Press, 1994.

Hyde, Margaret and Setaro, John. *Alcohol 101: An Overview For Teens.* Brookfield, Connecticut: Twenty-First Century Books, 1999.

Ketcham, Katherine and Pace M.D., Nicholas. *Teens Under the Influence: The Truth About Kids, Alcohol, and Other Drugs - How to Recognize the Problem and What to Do About It.* New York: Ballantine Books, 2003.

Klebanoff, Susan and Luborsky, Ellen. *Ups & Downs: How to Beat the Blues and Teen Depression.* New York: Price Stern Sloan, Inc., 1999.

Kuhn, C., Swartzwelder, S. and Wilson, W. *Buzzed: The Straight Facts About the Most Used and Abused Drugs From Alcohol to Ecstasy, Third Edition.* New York: W.W. Norton and Company, 2008.

Miller, J. W., Naimi, T. S., Brewer, R. D. and Jones, S. E. "Binge drinking and associated health risk behaviors among high school students." *Pediatrics* 2007; 119.

Miller, William R. and Heather, Nick (Eds). *Treating Addictive Behaviors: Processes of Change.* New York: Springer, 1986.

Mitchell, Hayley. *Teen Alcoholism.* San Diego, California: Lucent Books, 1998.

Nathan, Peter. "Environmental Interventions to Modify Rates of Binge Drinking and Proposed Interventions for Students After Beginning College." University of Iowa, 2005.

National Institute on Alcohol Abuse and Alcoholism. "A Snapshot of Annual High-Risk College Drinking Consequences" available at www.collegedrinkingprevention.gov/StatsSummaries/snapshot.aspx.

National Institute on Alcohol Abuse and Alcoholism. "Alcohol Poisoning" available at www.collegedrinkingprevention.gov/students/risky/alcoholpoisoning.aspx.

National Institute on Alcohol Abuse and Alcoholism. "NIAAA Council Approves Definition of Binge Drinking." *NIAAA Newsletter* 2004; 3:3.

National Institute on Alcohol Abuse and Alcoholism. "Steps for Effective Prevention Planning and Evaluation" available at www.collegedrinkingprevention.gov. NIAAACollegeMaterials/Handbook.

National Institutes of Health. "Tips For Cutting Down On Drinking." 2008; Publication No. 07-3769.

Office of Applied Studies. *The NSDUH Report: Alcohol Dependence or Abuse and Age at First Use.* Rockville, MD: Substance Abuse and Mental Health Services Administration, October 2004.

Savage, S. "27 Reasons Not to Serve (or Turn a Blind Eye To) Alcohol at High School Graduation Parties." *Dartmouth Center on Addiction, Recovery and Education*, 2005.

Seaman, Barret. *Binge: What Your College Student Won't Tell You.* New Jersey: John Wiley and Sons, 2005.

State of California. *California Driver Handbook. Text Alternative for BAC/DUI Chart.* Sacramento, California: 2009.

Stressfocus. "Adolescent Stress - It Can Cause Adverse Effect in the Future" available at www.stressfocus.com/stress_focus_article/teen-stress-causes.htm.

Substance Abuse and Mental Health Services Administration. *A Comprehensive Plan for Preventing and Reducing Underage Drinking.* Washington, DC: Supt. of Docs., U.S. Govt. Print. Off., 2006.

The Harm Reduction Network, Inc. "Alcohol Harm Reduction for College Students" available at www.collegedrinking.org.

University of Colorado Department of Alcohol and Drug Prevention and Education. *Numeric Blood Alcohol Level Chart.* University of Colorado.

University of Michigan Institute for Social Research. *2005 Monitoring the Future Study* available at www.monitoringthefuture.org.

U.S. Department of Health and Human Services. *Alcohol Alert - Changing the Culture of Campus Drinking.* Washington, D.C.: Supt. of Docs., U.S. Govt. Print. Off., 2002.

U.S. Department of Health and Human Services. *Alcohol Alert - Underage Drinking: Why Do Adolescents Drink, What Are the Risks, and How Can Underage Drinking Be Prevented?* Washington, D.C.: Supt. of Docs., U.S. Govt. Print. Off., 2006.

U.S. Department of Health and Human Services. *Alcohol Alert - Young Adult Drinking.* Washington D.C.: Supt. of Docs., U.S. Govt. Print. Off., 2006.

U.S. Department of Health and Human Services. SAMHSA's Center for Substance Abuse Prevention. *Prevention Alert: The Binge Drinking Epidemic.* Washington, DC: U.S. Government Printing Office 2002; 5(6).

U.S. Department of Health and Human Services. Substance Abuse and Mental Health Services Administration (2002, September 4). *Results from the 2001 National Household Survey on Drug Abuse: Volume 1.* Summary of National Findings (Office of Applied Studies, NHSDA Series H-17ed.) (BKD461, SMA 02-3758) Washington, DC: U.S. Government Printing Office.

U.S. Department of Health and Human Services. Substance Abuse and Mental Health Services Administration (2002, September 3). *Results from the 2001 National Household Survey on Drug Abuse: Volume II.* Technical Appendices and Selected Data Tables Series H-18 (Office of Applied Studies, NHSDA Series H-18 ed.) (BKD462, SMA 02-3759) Washington, DC: U.S. Government Printing Office.

U.S. Department of Health and Human Services. *The Surgeon General's Call to Action to Prevent and Reduce Underage Drinking.* Rockville, MD: U.S. Department of Health and Human Services, 2007.

Volkmann, Chris and Volkmann, Toren. *From Binge to Blackout: A Mother's Struggle with Teen Drinking.* New York: New American Library, 2006.

WebMD. "Anxiety & Panic Disorders Guide" available at www.webmd.com/anxiety-panic/guide/generalized-anxiety-disorder.

WebMD. "Depression Guide" available at www.webmd.com/depression/guide/teen-dpression.

WebMD. "Stress Management Health Center" available at www.webmd.com/balance/stress-management/stress-management.

Wechsler, H., Davenport, A., Dowdall, G.W., Moeykens, B. B. and Castillo, S. "Health and Behavioral Consequences of Binge Drinking in College: A National Survey of Students on 140 Campuses." *Journal of the American Medical Association* 1994; 272.

Wechsler, H., Dowdall, G. W., Davenport, A. and Castillo, S. "Correlates of College Student Binge Drinking." *American Journal of Public Health* 1995; 85.

Wechsler, H., Lee, J. E., Kuo, M., Seibring, M., Nelson, T. F. and Lee, H. "Trends in College Binge Drinking During a Period of Increased Prevention Efforts: Findings from 4 Harvard School of Public Health Surveys, 1993-2001." *Journal of American College Health* 2002; 50(5).

Wechsler, Henry and Wuethrick, Bernice. *Dying to Drink: Confronting Binge Drinking on College Campuses.* Emmaus, PA: Rodale Press, 2002.

Weitzman, E. R. "Social Developmental Overview of Heavy Episodic or Binge Drinking Among U.S. College Students." *Psychiatric Times* 2004; 21:2.

Weitzman, E. R. and Nelson, T. F. "College Student Binge Drinking and the 'Prevention Paradox': Implications for Prevention and Harm Reduction." *Journal of Drug Education* 2004; 34(3).

CPSIA information can be obtained at www.ICGtesting.com

231600LV00002B/65/P